From
Story Idea
to
Reader

Patsy Collins

&

Rosemary J. Kind

Printed in the United Kingdom

First Printing, 2016 Alfie Dog Limited

The authors can be contacted at: authors@alfiedog.com

ISBN: 978-1-909894-32-7

Published by:

Alfie Dog Limited

Schilde Lodge, Tholthorpe,
North Yorkshire, YO61 1SN
Tel: 0207 193 33 90

CONTENTS

ACKNOWLEDGMENTS

Patsy and Rosemary would like to express their thanks to *Writing Magazine*. They first met through the magazine's forum 'Talkback'. In addition to that, some of both Patsy's and Rosemary's material for this book originated as articles written for *Writing Magazine*.

They are also grateful to Suzy, Sheila, Jan and Lynne who form the other members of their critique group. Without their support and encouragement many of their writing projects would never see the light of day.

SECTION 1

INTRODUCTIONS

QUIZ

Important factors for a writer

Let's start with a quiz to get you thinking. On the page below, decide which factors you think are important in a writer and which might get in the way. After reading the book, come back and check whether your view has changed.

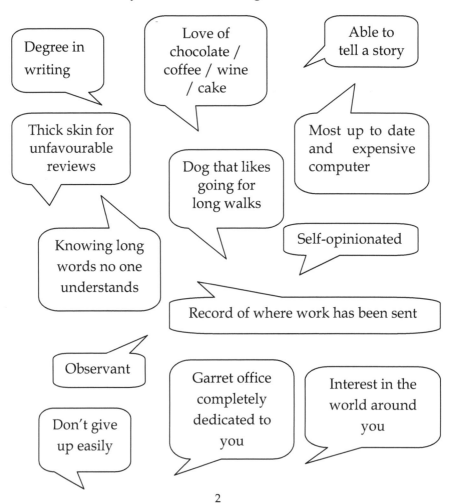

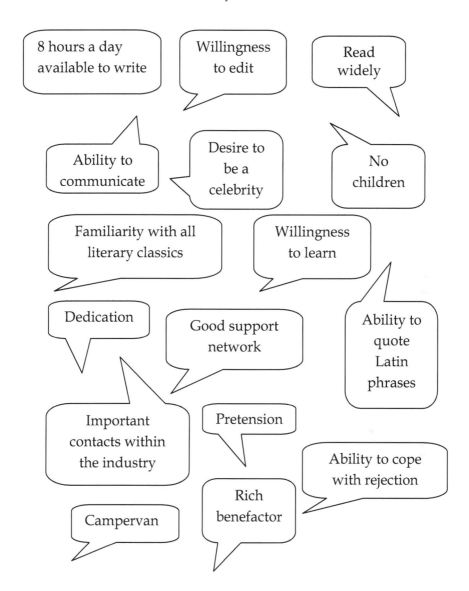

ANYONE CAN BECOME A BETTER WRITER

It is common to hear people say writing is not something you can learn. We don't agree. We believe anyone with the determination to improve their skills can, with practice, do exactly that. You may not be the next Booker prize winner, but, in time, you can hope to achieve a reasonable level of success.

As with everything, if you have a natural talent, then you have a head start. But, if you are willing to study the craft of writing and apply what you've learned, then with practice, and revision, your work will become better and better. Every writer needs to read widely and learn from the different styles of other writers. That's not to say you will always think their work is good and seek to emulate it. We can learn as much from the things we see flaws in, as we do from the things we aspire to.

> Every writer needs to read widely

Just because grammar wasn't taught when you were in school, doesn't mean you can't pick up a reference book or search on the internet to understand the basic rules. Grammar scares many writers, but, if you read the section later in the book, you'll begin to shatter the myth that you can't do it.

Reading a piece of high-brow fiction and saying, 'I can't do that,' and putting your pen down is the wrong place to start. You do not need over-complicated language. You need language your readers will understand and appreciate and a style relevant to that language. Focus on the story rather than on trying to 'impress' with long words and complicated phrases.

Be realistic in your writing goals. For one thing, remember that at school you start with the basics and work up. Very few of us would start studying for a degree in primary school. Take learning the craft of writing in the same bite-sized chunks and you will be surprised what you achieve in a relatively short time.

One of the problems you face when you start a writing career is, because 'writing' is something learned at school, many assume they already know how to do it. Whilst there are some very good school English teachers, not many teach you to look for stronger verbs rather than throwing in a plethora of adverbs, or explain to you what a 'story arc' actually means. Writing a good story for publication may need a little more development than you applied in your GCSE or O Level English.

We hope the following pages will give you the confidence to believe that, with practice, you can be an effective writer in your chosen genre. You're going to need a fair amount of dedication and a support network to encourage you, but we'll help you finding those as well. Whilst you are reading this book, take the time to practice all you learn along the way. It is intended to be a practical guide rather than a theoretical one, but the hard work is down to you!

Take the time to practice

INTRODUCTIONS

Patsy Collins

PC: Stories have always been part of my life. Dad invented them for me and my brother, and did all the voices. Nobody who's met him is shocked his daughter uses words for a living. Thanks to Mum I was amongst the first in my class to progress from 'John has a blue ball' to proper stories. The first books we shared were light-hearted escapist romance. My grandmothers, who played a large part in my childhood, were both avid readers of cosy crime and magazines such as *My Weekly*.

It's probably no coincidence much of my writing is dialogue heavy, that I write short fiction for women's magazines, and light-hearted escapist romances with a touch of crime. Perhaps less obvious is my route to publication.

I left school at sixteen with the O levels which are still my highest academic qualification. Over the following twenty years, I read loads and sometimes made up daft stories to amuse friends and colleagues. It's unlikely my boss actually believed the alien abduction tale, but she did forgive me arriving twenty minutes late that day.

Writing never occurred to me. It was something other people did. The kind of people who know the difference between a dangling modifier and split infinitive. Then stuff happened. Some of it not very cheery. As a result, I was living alone, for the first time ever, and in a new area.

What I needed was something to fill time, occupy my mind, help me meet people... and it had to be cheap. Creative writing classes were the answer. The brilliant tutor encouraged us to submit our work. In my first year, I had a couple of letters published and won book tokens and cake. Naturally I was hooked.

Since then, I've sold hundreds of short stories, mainly to women's magazines. I've won competitions, one of which resulted in the publication of my first novel. I write articles for *Writing Magazine* and of course there's this book. During this time, I've learned and improved a great deal. But I'm still going to leave explaining grammar to Rosemary.

For more about my writing visit www.patsycollins.uk and for my life in general see www.patsy-collins.blogspot.co.uk.

Rosemary J. Kind

RJK: I write because I have to. You could take almost anything away from me except my pen and paper. Failing to stop after the book that 'everyone has in them', I have gone on to publish books in both non-fiction and fiction, the latter including novels, humour, short stories and poetry. I also regularly produce magazine articles in a number of areas and write regularly for the dog press.

As a child I was desolate when, at the age of ten, my then teacher would not believe that my poem based on *Stig of the Dump* was my own work and I stopped writing poetry for several years as a result. I was persuaded to continue by the invitation to earn a little extra pocket money 'assisting' others to produce the required poems for English homework!

Always one to spot an opportunity, I started school newspapers and went on to begin providing paid copy to my local newspaper at the age of sixteen.

For twenty years I followed a traditional business career, before seeing the error of my ways and leaving it all behind to pursue my writing full-time.

I spend my life discussing plots with the characters in my head and with my faithful dogs, who generally put the opposing arguments when there are choices to be made.

Always willing to take on challenges that sensible people regard as impossible, I set up the short story download site Alfie Dog Fiction in 2012 and built it into being one of the largest in the world, representing over 300 authors and carrying over 1600 short stories. My hobby is developing the Entlebucher Mountain Dog in the UK and when we brought my beloved Alfie back from Belgium he was only the tenth in the country.

I started writing *Alfie's Diary* as an internet blog the day Alfie arrived to live with us, intending to continue for a year or two. Ten years later it goes from strength to strength and has repeatedly been named as one of the top ten dog blogs in the UK.

For more details you can find me at www.rjkind.co.uk. For more details about my dogs then you're better visiting www.alfiedog.me.uk.

Note

Throughout the book we have used the initials PC for Patsy and RJK for Rosemary. The initials are only used where there is a change of author.

GETTING STARTED – WHAT YOU NEED

PC: The quiz at the beginning of the book is a mixture of a few things we believe are needed by writers, some we think may be useful and others which, although sometimes considered desirable, are rather frivolous. It's a long list and could easily have been longer. The good news is that very little of this is needed straight away. To start writing all you need is the equipment to physically write with and the willingness to give it a go.

Pen and paper

You don't have to start by buying anything expensive.

> Keep pen and paper handy

Every writer, who can physically write and read what they've written, needs a pen and paper. Any pen, and the envelopes your bills arrive in will do to start with. Get into the habit of saving any usable paper and collecting any pens you find. Have a good supply wherever you expect to do most of your writing. Carry spares in any bags you use. Leave some at work, in the car, with any hobby or sports equipment, and in the shed on the allotment.

RJK: Next to the bed!

PC: I gave up on that, but yes some people find it helpful.

If you can, get hold of a decent pen for most of your writing. It needn't be expensive; big fat fountain pens with gold nibs look nice, but they can also be messy and uncomfortable to use. A ball point which flows freely and doesn't make your fingers ache might be a better choice.

Scrap paper is great for jotting down ideas and writing first drafts. You probably won't be able to get hold of enough to write a novel, but don't rule it out. When the organisation I was working for fifteen years ago rebranded, I asked for all their old headed stationary and was offered dozens of boxes. I haven't used it all yet.

Photocopy paper is the cheapest to buy. A ream (144 sheets) of A4 is about £2.99 in office supply stores, or less if you buy several packs at once. Sometimes you can find it in pound shops (dollar stores). Don't ask me what it costs there – I've heard that one before. Just buy the cheapest you can get which isn't too flimsy to work with comfortably.

Notebooks or exercise books might be more convenient, especially if you don't always write in the same place.

Words

You'll use a lot of these, so get in a good stock. Reading is an excellent way to collect them, so is listening to people (they don't have to be talking to you). Both sources also give hints about how to connect the words together.

Listen to people

Get a dictionary and use it. A small cheap one is fine, as is an old one from a charity shop.

Special cases

For most people, pen, paper and a bit of enthusiasm are all that's needed to make a start. For others it's not so easy. If you're blind, or can't physically hold a pen, then you'll need equipment to help you. A computer with software which can turn your spoken words into type, or read back what you type might well be the answer. There's also the possibility of dictating to a machine or another person and having the words typed for you. If required there's computer equipment which will transform eye movements into text or speech (as used by Professor Stephen Hawking).

If you already have something along these lines persevere with that until you've been writing for a while and know exactly what you'll want. It'll take up time to master any new equipment; time which will have been wasted if it doesn't suit your needs. Also technology advances quickly and in relative terms prices tend to drop, so waiting might well give you more options. Of course when I say 'waiting' I mean writing.

It's all just writing

Some people, I'm one of them, simply prefer to type than to write by hand. If you're the same and already have a computer, word processor, even a typewriter, then use that. If not, please don't put off making a start with your writing until you can buy one.

When we talk about writing in this book, we mean writing by hand, typing, dictation or any other method of recording words so they can be edited and read later on.

I firmly believe that whatever you already have is what you

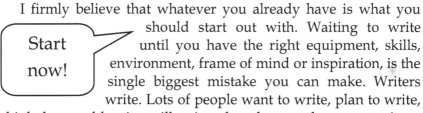 should start out with. Waiting to write until you have the right equipment, skills, environment, frame of mind or inspiration, is the single biggest mistake you can make. Writers write. Lots of people want to write, plan to write, think they could write, will write when they get the opportunity... some of them will, but until they actually put words on paper or machine they aren't writers.

Skills and qualifications

The ability to move words from your brain into a format you and others can access is vital. To get started, that's all you need. Terrible spelling, lack of punctuation and abysmal grammar can be corrected as you learn and you start learning as soon as you begin to write. The same applies to the techniques of storytelling; building suspense, bringing characters to life, creating an emotional response in the reader and everything else which will make your words worth reading. If there are areas where you don't have natural talent, then you can learn.

Most writers continue to learn and improve for as long as they keep writing (Rosemary and I have learned quite a bit from each other whilst writing this book) and you'll need to put in the time and effort to do this, but you can't learn to write without actually writing, so make a start.

Somewhere to write

You can scribble in a notebook on the bus going to work, or in a café, on the kitchen table, in the library... Honestly, you can write anywhere.

> Write wherever you are

In case I haven't been clear

The most important thing is the understanding that to be a writer you need to write. Anything you do which isn't actually writing... well, it's not actually writing is it? Just get the pen and put the pointy end onto a piece of paper and start writing.

EXERCISES

Throughout the book, we've included short exercises, encouraging you to try out the techniques and ideas we've introduced. Do give them a try, even if it's just a few scribbled lines, as they'll help you learn and remember what you've read. Better yet, try to work some of them up into complete stories which you can submit or enter into competitions.

EXERCISE

Write down one of your writing aspirations. Perhaps it's to get to grips with the punctuation required when writing dialogue, your first publication, or to finish your novel. Pin it up somewhere you'll see it regularly and make sure you work towards achieving it – by writing!

SECTION 2

WHAT TO WRITE

WRITING MORE THAN YOU ALREADY KNOW

No two lives are the same

PC: 'Write what you know' is fine if you have an exciting lifestyle or write kitchen sink dramas, but no use if your life is ordinary, or your chosen genre is science fiction or fantasy, is it? Well actually yes, it is.

What's ordinary for one person is novel to others. Being an only child, or having no family is a different experience from growing up with siblings or surrounded by a large extended family. The French film *Amelie* uses the loneliness felt by singletons to good effect. How the sisters interact is important in *Little Women*. *Dr Who* seeks human companions and becomes involved in protecting Earth because he's the last of his species. Mycroft Holmes adds depth to stories about his brother Sherlock.

> What's ordinary for one person is novel to others

Notes about how much your little brother annoyed you, or longing for a sister to gossip with, probably won't make a great novel on their own, but could form the backstory for a fascinating character.

Having a repetitive, boring job differs from the stresses of a role with the emergency services or the worries and frustrations of unemployment. All could spark an entertaining or compelling story. Walter Mitty and Reggie Perrin reacted against the tedium of their lives by retreating into fantasy. *The Full Monty* shows how unemployment impacts on a person's entire life. Obviously if your day job means there's more adrenaline in your blood, than caffeine in mine, it can be put to use in your

> Use what you already know

writing. The trick is to use what you already know, but adapt it and present it in a fresh way, so although some elements will be familiar to the reader, the story will be new.

Your unique experience

Jockey Dick Francis set his detective stories around stables and race courses. Andy McNab uses his experience in the British Army in his novels. Although to most people covert operations or riding past the winning post at thirty miles an hour sounds exciting, to McNab and Francis they were just part of the day job. Any stable lad or army trainee will recognise many details as a familiar part of their world. I grew up on a farm, so it's probably no surprise that one of my novels, *Escape to the Country*, is set somewhere similar. What might be more surprising is that I'd been writing for eight years and nodded my head countless times on hearing the advice to 'write what you know' before it occurred to me that a life which seemed so normal to me might make an interesting setting.

These stories aren't autobiographical; writing only what you know leaves you in danger of having just one story to tell. I'm sure Francis didn't discover a murdered body every time he put on his silks, I've never been rescued by a dishy tractor driver and even McNab must have had the odd dull day during his military service, but such things needn't limit the author. We start with what we know and build on it.

> Build on what you know

A touch of reality makes a story believable

What if your life really is 'normal'? The first Harry Potter book starts with two people who're proud to be normal. They have a normal house and Mrs. Dursley does a very normal (to me anyway) thing of spying on the neighbours. They worry about what other people

> A touch of reality makes a story believable

think. On page two the child has a tantrum; as a mother J. K. Rowling almost certainly experienced that. Later in the book Harry has the uncertainty of a new school and making new friends, as well as dealing with people who dislike him. Again these are things Rowling probably knows about. She adapted them to fit into a world where the school building can move, the pupils are learning magic and the friends and enemies might put a spell on the characters at any moment. Starting the book with a situation most readers will identify with helps make the rest believable.

Our home town, even our flat, could be the setting for a story; perhaps contemporary, or just after the first brick was laid 200 years ago, or after the apocalypse. Knowing the layout helps make the story believable and is useful for consistency. The bathroom won't suddenly switch floors or change size unless we want it to. That door which sticks, the creaking stair or stained carpet can be included to make story locations feel like real, lived in places rather than photos from a magazine.

RJK: The locations in my novel *The Appearance of Truth* are fictitious, but as I describe them I have used many places which are known to me. If you go for the walk around Billingbrook with Lisa and Pete, you'll encounter the park I played in as a child, the railway behind a friend's house and the nursery I went to for a while, amongst others. All sorts of every day experiences can be commandeered for use in other ways.

Keep the detail – Change the setting

Keep the detail – change the setting

PC: Small details work as part of a bigger story. If we go through a security procedure to get into our place of work, we could describe how the keypad feels, or the sound the swipe card makes when our character tries to rob a bank, or break into a top secret military base or his lover's flat. Most of us are faced with paperwork from time to time, just as James Bond is when accepting a new piece of equipment from Q branch.

If we've worked on a supermarket checkout, or queued

observantly at one, then we can write about working in a tiny boutique or huge department store or a newsagent's kiosk on a space ship. Just swap the trouble with scanning beans to difficulty with the bar code for a gimp mask or gravity defying pencil. Small, familiar details help the reader feel at home in an unfamiliar world.

Your past can become a character's present

Don't restrict yourself to using what you know just once. I used to be a tour guide on HMS Victory. That required learning a lot of history. I could have used the knowledge to write historical fiction, or a non-fiction historical piece, or an article on tourist attractions in Portsmouth, or put the eerie creakings the ship made when the public left into ghost stories.

Initially it might not seem such a job would have been any help with my usual writing, short fiction for women's magazines, but I've sold two stories about tour guides (set elsewhere) and one from the viewpoint of a visitor to the ship. True it wasn't a common job, but to me it was perfectly normal, much more so than working in a school, library or bank.

Whatever job we have it's something different from the vast majority of other people's experience. Don't forget there's more to our jobs than whatever we're paid to do. Many of my stories are inspired by events in the staff room, snatches of overheard conversation from visitors and things which occurred on my journey home.

> Every working experience is unique

If you've suffered a medical problem you could inflict it on your character, or write about one of the professionals caring for you, or your visitors. You could pen a sensationalist 'true life' account of your procedure, a poem using the rhythm of the saline drip, or a murder novel set on the ward. Perhaps your story will be set in the past where what's now a minor problem was a life threatening condition, or in the future where people or medical knowledge have evolved so much that your illness no longer exists, or is re-introduced as a modern plague. You'll have to make up most of it, but a detailed description of the symptoms could get you started. (If you've never been ill, consider a self-help piece on healthy living!)

If you need to know more… Do more!

> Get out there and try it!

Do you want to write convincingly about something you've never experienced? The answer here is to research, perhaps even go so far as 'Method Writing', like method acting but for writing – putting yourself into the situation. If that's a step too far, then just learn enough for the kind of convincing details which allow your reader to suspend disbelief.

Maybe you can't spend months familiarising yourself with an exotic location, but it might be possible to take a short break there. Failing that, talk to people who have visited, and read all you can about the place. Don't stick to the glowing reports in travel brochures. Look at websites which allow visitors to post negative comments, read accounts of people who've lived or worked in the area and view pictures which show more than tourist attractions. The website www.360cities.net is excellent as it shows all round views, giving the feeling you're in the scene rather than peering through a camera.

RJK: At a more local level Rightmove is a great way to find out what houses are like in a particular area and Google Street View is a very

> Make the most of the internet

good way to get a feel for a local setting. I wanted to know the layout of a house on a particular road to set a murder there and make it authentic; the internet provided everything I needed to know.

PC: You could research local plants and see them in botanic gardens, so you can write, with knowledge, about the colours, scents and textures. Visit appropriate restaurants or cook local dishes at home and put yourself in your character's place as you experience the flavours.

Whilst we're talking about eating, find an antique recipe book and recreate an appropriate dish for your historical drama, or concoct an amazing new dessert for your fantasy epic, or buy yourself the kind of boil in the bag gunk that'll add authenticity to your war or survival story. Whoever and whenever they are, your characters will almost certainly eat and you can act as their taster.

Seeking out new experiences

Look out for workshops and experience days or consider evening classes or voluntary work to gain an insight into subjects you'd like to write about. Offer to walk a neighbour's dog (RJK: or borrow one of mine!) and write about owning one, or stroking the hair on a Martian Furry-fluff-ferret. If your character must give evidence after witnessing a death, it's not practical to tail people who look likely to die suddenly, hoping to be called as a witness, but you can attend an inquest. It's something I did when writing my novel, *Paint Me a Picture*. Many court cases are open to the public and there are a huge range of public meetings. Go to some. Talk to protesters and the people who want to tell you about Jesus or double glazing, if those subjects are of interest to your character.

> Evening classes and voluntary work can be useful

You might not want to give birth to sextuplets to write about a world where that's the norm, or kidnap children to write about life as a slave trader, or canoe a bunch of them down the Nile for your epic adventure story, but you could hold a sleepover for your children's friends to get some insight. The same thing might be useful research for a horror story.

> Ask questions and note answers

Never turn down what could be a fascinating learning experience. Every time you go somewhere new, meet a person from a different background or do something you've never attempted before, you're increasing the range of things you can write about with a certain amount of authority.

Write what you know, but don't stop there. Adapt and expand

what you know. Learn more. Soon you'll be writing more than you ever thought possible.

EXERCISE

Compare some of your life experiences with friends or members of your writing group and note areas of difference. Could you use those things as a backdrop for a story? Also note any unusual experience they have – perhaps you could build another story around that.

RJK: You can use the above technique whenever you meet new people, even sitting next to them on a bus, train or plane. You will be amazed at the ranges of experience you can find just by letting people talk about themselves. Train yourself to always ask yourself as you are listening, 'How could I use this in a story?'.

101 SOURCES OF WRITING IDEAS

1. PC: You don't need to look further than your own life for inspiration for anything from a filler about one moment, to an autobiography describing your whole history. You can keep it factual, gloss over the truth or embellish with fictional details, depending on your market. It's also possible to write short stories based on real experiences.

2. Other people's lives are interesting too. Biographic writing can focus on one decisive event, or an entire life. The subject needn't be famous. Family members or local characters might have fascinating stories to tell. Perhaps you'll create a biography or autobiography as a record for your grandchildren.

3. Newspaper headlines can be great story prompts, especially if you avoid reading the rest of the article.

   Newspaper headlines

4. Or write your own news report. Local papers often welcome, though seldom pay, someone willing to provide a write-up of sports matches, fêtes and events.

5. Talk to a homeless person. How did they end up in that situation? It might be worth buying them a cup of tea and sandwich to find out. You could write up the answer, or something inspired by it, a plea to help, or a piece to help others avoid such a situation.

6. Make a note of your suspicions if you witness unusual behaviour. Record what happened and your thoughts and reactions, before the innocent explanation spoils a promising plot-line.

7. Reading the lonely heart ads reveals interesting characters. Try putting them together in likely, or unlikely, combinations.

8. Studying problem pages could also be inspiring. How did

they get into that mess? Will the person follow the advice? Will it help? Or maybe you could write a self-help piece for others with similar issues.

9. Accidentally overhear people's conversations on the High Street and continue them in your imagination, or write what led up to the bit you heard. Do watch out for lamp posts as you trail behind scribbling notes... And those A boards listing special offers outside shops... And small dogs on extendable leads.

10. Free ads. People sell some strange things. Who'd buy them and why?

11. Dropped items or lost property. What happened to the man who lost that shoe? How did the child react when she discovered teddy was missing? What was done to retrieve the lost item? Maybe someone was glad to see the back of it.

> Lost property

12. The supermarket. It's not quite as simple as finding the aisle for your chosen genre and selecting by word length, but ideas are there. Do customers need all that stuff? Can they afford it? Are they in a hurry or not?

13. Charity shops. Who owned that interesting looking item. Why don't they want it anymore?

14. While we're out shopping, have a look at car boot sales. Is anyone selling murder weapons, cursed china, their wife's favourite ornament?

15. Compare the differences in people's expressions as they enter and leave: the dentist, beauty salon, betting shop, slimming club, that mysterious establishment with blacked-out windows...

16. Notice people's clothes, especially unusual combinations, or those which seem designed to blend in. What motivated those choices?

17. Graffitied walls. Why was Baz 'ere? What did he do? Why did he need to record his presence? And where is he now? Or maybe he wasn't there at all. Could it be a code?

> Graffiti

18. Park benches, or rather the dedications on them. Did Eric

really love this spot? Why? And why did his friends or family choose this one over other places which were important to him?

19. Watching birds or other wildlife in a nature reserve is a great way to relax and can provide story or article ideas. Doing this led to several scenes in my novel, *Firestarter*.

20. A fork in the path – what would have happened if you, or your character, had taken the other one?

21. Airports, taxi ranks, train stations. Where are people going? Who are they meeting? What have they left behind?

22. 22 On jetties and breakwaters. Whose ship is coming in? Is it bringing what they hoped for? Who'll sail out on it?

23. Car parks. Odd things go on. Trust me.

24. Under an umbrella. Talking about the weather is a national pastime. I've sold three short stories based on people doing just that. How about a self-help piece on dealing with extremes of weather or money-saving tips on keeping warm?

25. Weather trends, global warming or rainbows are all possible article, story, or poetry topics.

26. Search for online 'plot generators'.

27. Facebook and Twitter updates. What caused that online rant? What happened next?

28. Look at trending hashtags and combine them into a story.

> Trending hashtags

29. Write one of those quizzes to see what kind of cake a person resembles, or what their goldfish name would be.

30. Got an embarrassing rash or worried about a legal problem? Google to see what's the worst that could happen and you'll have the start of a horror story.

31. Scam emails. What's the purpose behind them? Is it achieved?

32. In bed. No, not erotica! Note down any interesting dreams you remember, or ideas which come to your subconscious when you're most relaxed.

33. Or you could write what you first thought of when I mentioned getting ideas in the bedroom. I don't know how

old the phrase 'sex sells!' is, but it's just as true now as when people first cottoned onto it.

34. Gravestones. Those with quotes, eulogies or mini family histories can be a good starting point. Take a look at the tributes left too.

> Gravestones

35. Obituaries. What do they say and what have they left out? Is that how everyone viewed the deceased or is someone shaking their head in disbelief?

36. Archaeology reports can provide fascinating details which could form the basis of a factual or speculative piece about that individual, or be incorporated into fiction.

37. Autopsy results prompted many of Kathy Reichs' best-selling novels.

38. Wills and last requests. Shakespeare left his second best bed to his wife, Houdini requested his wife hold an annual séance so he could visit her. John Bowman wanted his dinner prepared every night, in case he came back.

39. The Past. Straightforward historical fact or fiction is always popular.

40. Research your family tree. (RJK: Doing mine gave me the idea for a whole novel.)

41. PC: Read old diaries or letters; yours, great-great-grandma's, Queen Victoria's.

42. Historical crimes. Rewrite a murder, setting it in the present. 'Solve' a mystery or just use the characters in your own work.

43. A visit to a castle could result in useful material. There's one in Kent which I'm desperate to use as the setting for a murder.

44. Re-enactment events. Often people don't just dress in character, they act and talk that way too, so they're perfect for immersive research.

> Re-enactment events

45. Your memories. Write it how it was, or how you wish it had been, or even how you're glad it wasn't.

46. When you holiday abroad, you're also conducting a research trip. Straightforward, factual travel pieces are

always in demand. Or perhaps you could put a slant on your trip so it's suitable for a cookery or sporting publication. (RJK: Or set a story in the location to make the story seem more exotic.)

47. PC: That car driving at speed down the road, where's it going? How did it get that dent? What or who is the driver trying to escape from?

48. What's in that closely guarded handbag?

49. Keep watch on the house next door. Who are all those people who keep visiting? What was that row really about?

50. Pay attention in the Post Office too. What exactly is in those packages?

51. You don't need to believe them, but do read horoscopes. Write a story based on yours, or the effects of following or ignoring one. That's how I came up with my novel, *A Year And A Day*.

52. Other people's writing can be a source of inspiration. You can't use their characters or the world they've created, but you could use them as inspiration to create your own. A tooth fairy version of Hogwarts perhaps, or a 100 year old adventurer who breaks into an old people's home looking for a quiet life?

53. Classic, out of copyright, works can be retold. Fairytales, legends, even bible stories can be brought up to date, transformed into science fiction or the characters re-homed.

54. Rejection slips might not seem the obvious source of inspiration, but if they contain any feedback they can, and most definitely should, be taken into account if the piece is reworked.

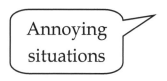

Annoying situations

55. In annoying situations. You could write a how-to piece on handling stress, or a fictionalised version of the situation and make it all come right for your characters, or become far worse, or a humorous piece ridiculing what happened.

56. Let off steam with a letter of complaint for poor goods or

services. This could be to get action or a refund, or as an open letter to be published.

57. Use your thirst for revenge and write the person who irritated you into a story and sort them out. I do that a lot.

58. Your non-writing brainwaves can be written up. Household hints and tips, especially with photos, are published by several magazines including *that's life!*, *Take a Break* and *Pick Me Up*. The rate per word is higher than for short stories or articles. Funny, true stories or opinion pieces are also welcomed.

59. Your good ideas or triumphs in the garden can also be sold as letters or fillers to numerous gardening magazines.

60. Your craft room or work basket could inspire a how-to piece on making a particular item or fiction based on your character's creativity.

61. Paintings. As with art, your writing could be surreal, modern or just plain odd. Perhaps, like Tracy Chevalier, you'd prefer to use a classic masterpiece.

62. Competitions. Many, including those in *Writing Magazine*, have a theme or prompt. You can use these for a story even if you don't plan to enter.

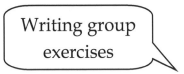

Writing group exercises

63. Writing group exercises. You each give a random word and then write a piece including as many as possible, or play a version of 'consequences' and fill out the resulting story outline. Swap stalled stories.

64. Titles. Book, story or song. Neither ideas nor titles are subject to copyright.

65. Song lyrics can prompt stories. You can't use the same words, nor any distinctive phrases or characters, but you can use the ideas or emotions they conjure up.

66. Ditto poems.

67. Your own stories. Try rewriting from a different point of view (POV), or change the ending.

68. What happens to people after they've had their few minutes of fame on the local TV news or if they're shown in the crowd when they were supposed to be elsewhere?

(RJK: Or with someone they should not have been with.)

69. PC: Picture postcards. Is the sender really having such a great time, or is trying to make you jealous the highlight of the trip?

70. Photos. Yours or someone else's. I've been told people use photos I post on www.patsy-collins.blogspot.com as story prompts.

> Photos

71. Down the back of the sofa. Yes, literally stick your hand down under the cushions and see what's there. It's tactful to wait until the owner has left the room and to replace your finds before they come back. (RJK: And wash your hands!)

72. PC: Your fears and…

73. Hopes. If either are filling your head to such an extent you can't think of anything else, then write about them.

74. In every disappointment. Rewrite events to cheer you up, or delve into how much worse it could have been; misery lit is still selling.

75. In the gaps. If your favourite publication has a gap in its coverage of whatever you're interested in, offer to fill it.

76. Book shops, newsagents and libraries. Find out the kind of stories people would like to read, or what they'd like to know, and write it for them.

77. At work. Whether it's the job itself, customers, clients or office politics there's bound to be something you can use.

78. The dictionary. Look up obscure words and bring them into use, or visit my blog for the Wednesday word of the week.

79. Lost in translation. Try watching a film or TV with the dialogue muted or in a language you don't understand and write your own story based on what you see. Only view for a few minutes though. You want to be inspired not plagiarise.

> The Attic

80. The attic. What's up there? Why was it kept, not thrown away?

81. Out of your comfort zone. Try a genre you've never written before.

82. The innocence of children. (Or their guilt.) They can ask great questions or make interesting observations. Look at the world through their eyes for a while. Or write about them repeating something they shouldn't have heard.

83. If you write non-fiction for adults, consider adapting your subject for children. Don't attempt this without good prior knowledge. You need to know a subject well to explain it simply.

84. Listen to someone speaking on the phone. Fill in the other part of the conversation.

85. Wrong numbers. Who did they really want to speak to? What distraction caused them to misdial, or perhaps they weren't given the correct number to start with. In that case, was yours given deliberately?

86. Before you pick up letters from the doormat, allow yourself to speculate about the possible contents.

87. Valentine's, Christmas, birthdays, anniversaries. The combination of hope, memories and expectation give almost endless emotional material to work with.

88. If you've ever been in love, or wanted to be, or are glad you're not, you have a story to tell.

89. Is the hospital patient alone? What's the nurse thinking about? Will scientific advances eradicate disease?

90. Take your character with you everywhere you go. Watch what they do, how they react, notice the things they'd notice.

91. On your keyboard. Often if you can just make yourself get started, the ideas will come.

92. If a straightforward story doesn't appeal, how about alternative writing forms such as an exchange of letters, emails or text messages?

This day in history

93. Look at 'this day in history' on the calendar. Even better, look a few months ahead so your piece is still topical after submission.

94. Sign posts and maps. Unusual place names are great for character names, or you can imagine what the place is like from the name alone.

95. If you have a pet then you have a source of inspiration, even if only for shaggy dog tales.

96. Transport yourself to the future. Will it be as Dystopian as George Orwell's *1984* or as amusing as the *Stainless Steel Rat* and *Hitchhiker's Guide to the Galaxy?*

97. Look around you next time you're at a wedding. Is everyone happy for the couple? Is the bridesmaid excited, the registrar bored, the photographer distracted?

98. Take a look at visitor books and websites such as Trip Advisor. Read between the lines to discover why the writer was so miserable, or delighted. *Visitor books*

99. In pretty paper. What was the sender of that unwanted gift thinking? Or create a non-fiction piece on what to do with them, or advice on how to avoid sending them.

100. In a panic. Although I've done it, I don't recommend this one. However, if you leave it to the last minute it's amazing how the pressure of a deadline can squeeze out ideas.

101. Anywhere you've got no means to write down the brilliant idea which has just come to you, seems to be a common location for inspiration to strike. Take a good memory and loiter.

EXERCISE

Select three of the items from the list above as sources of ideas and write at least 300 words inspired by each of them. (You can use these as pieces to edit as you work through other sections or to develop into full stories later.)

GENERATING IDEAS – MIND MAPPING

RJK: Before you start to generate your ideas, you need to decide the approach you are taking with your story. You can either start from the submissions guidelines and work from there, or you can start by developing the story and then decide where it would fit. If you are writing to submission requirements, either for a competition or a magazine, then start by asking yourself the following questions and note down your answers:

1. Who am I writing for? Who will be the readers? Patsy will say a lot more about this later.

2. Do the submissions guidelines or competition rules mention any taboo subjects or favoured topics?

3. How long should the story be?

4. Do the guidelines mention anything specific that should be included? An opening line, key words, etc.

Once you've gathered this information and, where appropriate, studied the market or the previous competition winning stories and judges, then you are ready to begin. For some writers this involves staring at a blank screen or sheet of paper for a long period of time, before declaring themselves to have 'writers' block' and giving up for the day. It really doesn't have to be that way!

A preformed idea

Sometimes a writer will tell you their story just came to them in its entirety; a whole plot occurred to them and all they had to do was write it down. That's the 5% inspiration and if you wait for that to happen before you put words on the

Who am I writing for?

Hard work not just inspiration

page, then you could be waiting a very long time. It is better to get something on the page that you can edit later than to write nothing, but that doesn't mean you have to start with sentences.

If your story is going to come from the other 95%, the perspiration rather than the inspiration, it's going to mean working hard. In the last section Patsy has explained there are many places you can get ideas from. Now it's time to take those ideas further and start to develop them into a story. I'm going to take two of those suggestions and show you how you can use mind maps and What If? scenarios to develop your story. Some people are more comfortable with one approach and some with the other. For me, Mind Maps are the ultimate safety net and you will rarely fail to generate a number of possible story options by using them.

What if?

I'm going to take number 63 from Patsy's list for this one. Years ago, I was part of a writing group which was given the task to write 300 words on the word 'Verisimilitude'. Fortunately, I keep a dictionary on my desk. Having looked up the precise meaning, 'having the appearance of truth', I looked around my desk for inspiration. (This probably takes us to point 1 on Patsy's list). At the time, I was researching my family tree and sitting on my desk was a birth certificate that I had sent away for. My thought process went as follows:

What if I got that birth certificate so I could pretend to be that person?

What if I'd grown up thinking that was really mine when it wasn't?

What if I suddenly found out my birth certificate was not my own and I didn't know who I was?

Suddenly I had all sorts of possibilities opening up. Whose certificate was it really? Why did they not need it anymore? Why would someone pass a child off as having a different identity?

From asking myself the very basic

question 'What if?' my thought path moved on step by step until 104,000 words later I had my novel, *The Appearance of Truth*, and it all came out of a one word writing exercise for a writing group. I'm not going to work up the mind map that would go with that particular idea as, inevitably, in doing so I would give away the plot of my novel and that might spoil it for you. However, we can move on to looking at how to generate a more visual and complete plotting method with another idea.

EXERCISE

Select an item from your desk and ask yourself as many 'What if?' questions as you can think of.

What if it had not been invented? What if it were to be used for a different purpose? What if you were an alien and had no idea what it was for? What if you were never going to be able to buy another one again? What if it had previously been owned by someone famous?

See just how many different scenarios you can come up with for a single object and how far you can develop the idea you come up with.

Mind mapping

Let's take point 10 from Patsy's list – a Free ad. The first item I found was a bicycle, so I have written that in the middle of my page. Of course, if you are like me you might have many odd notes jotted down and any one of them can work equally well. Around your central word put the standard five questions – How? Who? What? Where? When? Then one by one ask yourself those questions in relation to the word you've put in the middle, in this case 'bicycle'. Put down every answer you can think of around the question it relates to.

How?

How did the bicycle come to be in the free ads? – divorce, death, outgrown, used as a getaway 'vehicle', broken – these were the first things that came to my mind, so I have written those words around the 'How?'

Whose bicycle was it? – I've just put four possibilities here, own, daughter, father, friend, but you will be able to think of many more than this.

Who?

What?

What sort of bike is it? – I'm sure you can think of more than the five I've used to illustrate this. I've given a selection to show the wide variety of answers you might come up with. A tricycle with pink ribbons, a chopper, a unicycle, a mountain bike and an old fashioned bike with a basket. Unicycle might seem less obvious, but living in a village that had a unicycle hockey team as well as a unicycling juggling team (I kid you not) for me it is the first one to come to mind. Think as widely as you can when you do this exercise.

Where is the bicycle? – Think about diverse locations that it might be being sold from. An old people's home, a tower block, a shop and so on. Maybe it's not on Earth at all and is somewhere in outer space.

Where?

When?

When? – Again the possibilities are endless, but I've given four just to give you a flavour. If you use a past date you either need to be thinking time travel, or check that the type of bicycle you select existed then. I've also put a future date, Friday to make it immediate, and Christmas.

What you now have is a picture something like this:

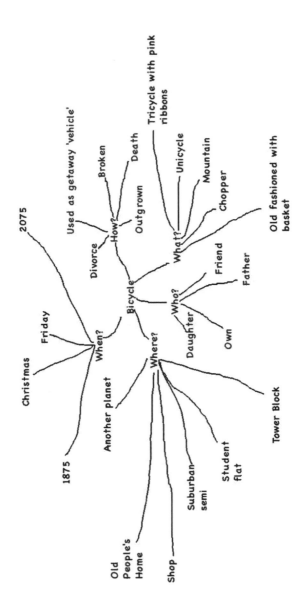

Now you move onto stage two of deciding what your story's components will be. Which you choose will form the basis of what you write. The beauty of your mind map is without knowing it, you have created the basis for many different stories just by varying the choices you now make. If I select the tricycle with pink ribbons, being sold as a result of the death of a daughter at Christmas from a suburban semi, I have the basis of an incredibly sad story telling of a tragedy or maybe a brave story of recognising that it's time to move on. For each component you select keep asking yourself Why? How? etc. and noting down what you think.

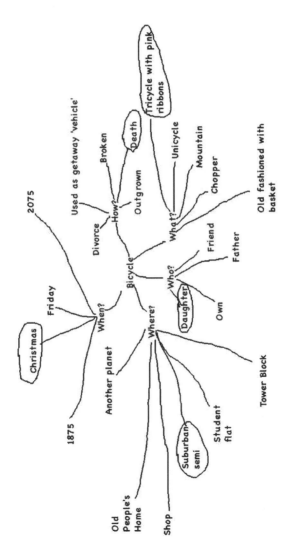

Why is it being sold at Christmas? Is the money needed for presents for those who are still alive? Is it just too painful to keep in the house for the festive season? How did the little girl die? Was she ill? Did she have an accident? Did she die doing something incredibly brave and saving someone else? When you keep doing this you can end up with quite literally thousands of ideas from a single mind map.

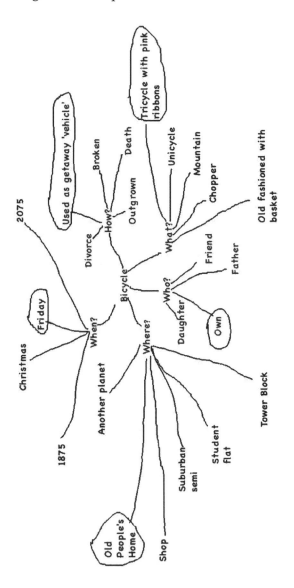

Maybe you want to write something humorous. You might still have selected the child's bike with the pink ribbons, but what about if it is being sold from an old people's home having been used as a getaway vehicle and is being sold by its owner? You can now start asking yourself what were they getting away from? How on earth did they fit on the bike? What happened?

The selection of the child's bike with ribbons being sold from an old people's home might also lead you to a very poignant story about the reversion to childhood by one of the residents.

Also, remember this is fiction you are writing, so if the items you have circled don't end up quite fitting the idea that starts to develop, then don't be afraid to vary them. This is your story, you can make it anything you want it to be.

PC: I've never drawn a mind map, but it sounds very like the mental process I go through when making up a short story, especially one based on a set prompt or topic.

EXERCISE

Take one of the 101 sources of writing ideas from the previous section and draw your own mind map based on it. When you've taken it as far as you want to go, choose a path through all the options to form the basis of a story.

WHICH PERSON TO WRITE IN?

First, second or third person?

RJK: When I'm talking about which person to write in, I don't mean Joe or Fred, we'll come back to that when we look at point of view. Here I mean 1st person (I), 2nd person (You) or 3rd person (He, She or It). Which of those will you choose for your narrative voice?

If you've studied languages you will probably be very familiar with the idea that verb endings can change according to whether you talk about I, you, he etc. Which you choose for your narrative voice will give a very different impression to the reader and may significantly change the style of the piece. I will go through each of them in turn in a moment. However, it is important to note that if you are writing for a specific market you need to be aware of their preference before you start writing your story. Some magazines favour one approach, some specifically say they don't like one or other option. It is of course possible to change a story you have written in the third person into a first person story at a later date, but don't underestimate how much work that can be. It is not as simple as using 'find and replace' in your word processing package and substituting 'I' for 'he'. We are back to changes to verb endings at the very least.

PC: It's good to experiment with this aspect (and others) but do make a decision during the first few drafts. Almost every sentence will need to be changed and sometimes there are story elements which either need to be rewritten or simply won't work in one form.

First person

RJK: Writing in the first person is very immediate. You can get deep into one character and very easily show their thoughts and deeds. Of course you can mislead the reader by having an unreliable first person; someone who lies compulsively for example. Your first person character may not know the whole truth themselves, a child or detective perhaps, and the reader may be led, by listening to conversations by other characters, to work things out before your protagonist does. It would not be the first time I've shouted at a character in a book, because they are being so slow in picking something up that they really need to know. One of the best examples of an unreliable narrator I know is in *Moriarty* by Anthony Horowitz, it's worth reading simply to get a grasp of how far you can take the concept.

> In first person it is less common to run into POV problems in a story

In first person it is much less common to run into point of view problems in a story, as it is very obvious that if the 'I' character is not there in a scene they cannot see what is going on and the story follows them much more closely. Writing in the first person can bring the reader closer to your character, but does not work for everyone and some magazines specifically avoid it in their stories.

Second person

Writing in the second person is a difficult one. When you are telling a story and say 'you did x', 'you thought y' you are putting all the thoughts and actions onto the reader. This can work if the reader is in a position to empathise with the situation and character they are being asked to identify with. I would caution against it in a story where the lead character is in any way the bad guy, or has repulsive behaviour that will alienate the reader. The risk is that as soon as you get to something that the reader most certainly would not do then, instead of remaining lost in the world you have created, they come out of the story and are mentally saying 'no I wouldn't', 'no I didn't'.

At that point you have lost your audience. A story where there is a twist at the end with the lead character having a deep character flaw is going to leave the reader feeling repulsed and unhappy with themselves. They are rarely going to want to come back to your writing for more. There is also an opposite to this, even if you make your character good and nice, if they are too sickly sweet, again you may find your reader cannot identify closely enough with the character and does not want to be addressed as 'you' throughout the story.

PC: This approach can be hard both to write and to read over an extended period. It can work well though, especially in short scenes. I wrote a twist ending short story in second person, in which the 'you' character was the bad guy. It was bought by two magazines, selected for audio publication and is now available from Alfie Dog Fiction. It was an exception, not something I'll do often.

Third person

RJK: Using third person, 'he' or 'she', or in some cases 'it' or 'they', gives the narrator a wider range of options in how the story can be shown. If you are using multiple viewpoint characters it is better to use third person. Switching between characters in first person is almost always very confusing for the reader. Bear in mind that 'he' or 'she' do not have to be human, they can work equally well for aliens, fantasy creatures and animals.

It is rare that a good story is written using 'it'. Stories from the point of view of an inanimate object have to be very special in order to work. Whilst they can be a good writing exercise, unless they offer something unique you will rarely find them accepted for publication.

> Stories from POV of an inanimate object have to be very special in order to work

One – formal

Unless you have been born into the higher echelons of society, or attended a rather expensive public school, it is unlikely that phrasing sentences using the more formal 'One' as the person of the sentence will come naturally. Inevitably, as it is more formal, using it will make the reader feel more distant from the character. However, if that is the desired effect, or if you are portraying a particular type of character then it might be appropriate.

PC: Can be used to add comedy or irony too.

Using them to good effect

RJK: Once you've understood the impact you can have by writing in each of the different persons, then you can decide how to use them most effectively to communicate your story.

> Writing in first person can make it difficult to show the range of events and characters

Writing solely in the first person can make it difficult to show the range of events and characters that are needed in a story and is the reason many writers shy away from it. It is perhaps easier in a short story than a novel. If you are using third person, you can more easily switch between characters in a novel (the extent of doing this in a short story should be limited). In a crime novel for example you may wish to switch between the activities of the murderer and those of the investigator. Clearly they can't be together all the time or there would be no story. Writing a crime novel in the first person takes away the potential to look effectively at both sides. You can tell it solely from the point of view of the investigation, but that restricts the methods that can be used to give the background story to the reader.

In theory, when writing a novel or story you should choose one of the persons (first, second or third – not a character!) and stick with it throughout the work. In practice there can be very good reason to break that rule. In my novel, *The Appearance of Truth*, most of the story is told in the third person from the point of view of the lead character, Lisa Forster. It is set in 2009 and follows her story. However, interspersed through the book are a number of chapters which go back to her 'mother' and the story of how she came to care for Lisa and all that led up to it. These chapters are in places deeply emotional. They are set in the 1970s and cover some very difficult incidents in Maureen's life. Because they are so clearly demarcated from the rest of the book, set apart in time as well as by who is the protagonist at that point; and because of the deeply emotional nature of those sections of the book, I chose to write those chapters in the first person. It breaks the rule for a reason and I think it works.

PC: Anything which works is the right thing to do.

RJK: It can be fun to experiment with which person to use, and writing the same story in each person can be a worthwhile exercise to assess the impact for yourself. Normally I would choose between first and third, unless there is a very good reason to the contrary.

EXERCISE

Take a short piece of work that you have written, or a section of a longer piece, and rewrite it in a different person. If it's in third person already, try seeing how it would look in first or second person. Compare them with the original to see which works best and whether they have a different effect on the reader.

MASTERING POINT OF VIEW

Whose story is this?

When you start writing any piece of fiction, you need to ask yourself 'Whose story is this?' That will usually determine whose point of view you are going to use within the work. You need to be able to convey a deeper understanding of your lead character and you do that by showing their thoughts and feelings.

Single point of view

Point of view (often referred to as POV) seems to be one of the hardest concepts for writers to grasp. You can look at your story in many ways, but let's start with a single first person point of view, as that is the easiest to understand. If you are writing in the first person (that's 'I' rather than he or she) then you are thinking as your character for the whole story. If your character does not see it happen, then you don't see it happen. If your character is not there, then you are not there. If the knowledge is not available to your character, then it is not available to you.

For example, imagine your character is in a room with two other people who they have never met before and have not been introduced to, a waiting room at the doctor's perhaps.

'I eased myself into the plastic bucket seat and looked around the nearly empty room. Mr. Smith and Mrs. Jones were clearly ahead of me in the queue.'

What's wrong with this? The character has used the names of the other patients, but as far as the reader has been led to believe these are complete strangers to him, so he cannot know their names. He would have to say, '… a man and a woman were clearly ahead of me…' The only way you can avoid that is if the receptionist has addressed the others in the room by name, so the patient has heard what they are called.

Continuing with this scenario, your patient, let's call him Fred, can't know what Mr. Smith or Mrs. Jones are thinking. He can say 'the man fidgeted, looking repeatedly at his watch' or if you are resorting to telling 'the man looked bored'. What he cannot know is that the man 'was' bored. Fred doesn't know what the other man is feeling, he can only know what he himself is thinking and make observations based on what he sees and hears.

Once Fred goes through into the Doctor's surgery, then at that point he is cut off from the waiting room. When he closes the door he can no longer see anything of what is happening in the waiting room. For all he knows Mrs. Jones may have removed all her clothes and be dancing naked around the room, but Fred cannot mention it as he cannot see it and does not know it is happening. If you want to cover the activity, it either has to be loud enough for Fred to hear and surmise what is going on, or someone needs to come in and tell them. Without either of those he can only hear about it later from someone who was there or who had themselves heard about it.

In the same way, Fred, unless it is clear he knows of Mr. Smith or Mrs. Jones and has heard gossip, cannot introduce any background about these characters as it is information to which he is not privy. He may be able to make some assumptions based on their appearances or what they are carrying, in the way of Sherlock Holmes, in which case it should be made clear that they are merely his deductions, which could of course be wrong.

As the writer, you must write it as though you are Fred and you see, know, hear, feel, only what Fred sees, knows, hears or feels and nothing else. There might be times, particularly in a longer work, that you introduce other points of view, but in a short story it is generally best to stick with one character, so as not to confuse the reader and so that you make it a deeper more realistic experience.

When you do change POV, do so deliberately and for a definite reason

PC: When you do change POV, do so deliberately and for a definite reason. Doing so randomly is head hopping and that is very, very bad.

RJK: POV is one of the things that many writers find difficult. It is also one of those things that you really have to understand before you can break the rules and make it work. I've talked before about writing in the first person, that is the easiest way to keep the point of view straight. It is fairly straightforward to comprehend that if you are writing as that person you can only see, think, feel the things that they do and not what is happening in the head of another character. However, what about writing in the third person?

My narrator is telling a story, surely he can tell anything he wants to can't he? Well, that depends on who your narrator is. If he is one of your characters then no, he can't tell you everything. As with the first person, that narrator can only tell you what he is conscious of or what is reported to him. If your narrator is omniscient, then yes, in theory he could portray all POVs and all feelings, but why would you want to do this?

If you look at the story from the reader's perspective, what do you want the reader to get out of it? The best reading experiences are when you can deeply identify with the protagonist. You can get behind them and cheer for them. You can cower with them when they are scared. Your heart can race when they face danger or passion. You can cry for them when things go wrong and laugh with them when they are amused. You come away from the story convinced you know the person. Sometimes, the impact is so great that for a while it is almost confused in your mind if they are a real person you know, or a character from the book you've read.

PC: It can feel that way when writing too!

RJK: You rarely come away with that feeling where an omniscient narrator is used or where some sort of hybrid switching between multiple characters has occurred. You only get that level of 'bonding' where the narrator limits themselves to one, or very few, points of view.

Where a writer insists on giving multiple POVs, they must at the very least be separated by the start of a new paragraph. 'Head hopping' within a paragraph is very confusing to the reader and can leave them feeling bewildered and at worst

> Changes of POV must be separated by the start of a new paragraph

too dizzy to read on. It must, at all times, be clear to the reader who is saying or doing what. Otherwise they will spend time going back over pages to work it out and come out of the story in the process.

If you are narrating from one point of view, you need to remember some key points. If that character leaves the room, you cannot continue to report what is going on inside. If he stands outside and listens, you may be able to continue to report sound, but unless he has his eye to the keyhole or the crack in the hinge then he cannot see what is happening. If another character shivers your narrator can't know 'Joe felt cold'. Fred (the viewpoint character) cannot know what Joe is feeling. You can say 'Joe appeared to feel cold' or 'Joe shivered and Fred wondered if he should turn up the radiator.'

An illustration of point of view

The following is a passage from the first chapter of my novel, *The Appearance of Truth*. This part is in Lisa's point of view. We find out what she is thinking and feeling but not the equivalent for the other character in the scene (Pete). I've added annotations in italics and brackets to show you what I mean.

> "Sorry. I'm sorry," she sobbed and went to move round him. She blew her nose on another scrappy old tissue from her coat pocket and tried to regain some composure. *(We can know that she is trying to regain composure because it is her POV – we could not know this about the other character. If it were about him we might say 'he appeared to try to regain composure')* It was a gusty day and she felt *(she is the viewpoint character so we can know what she feels)* the wind driving a tear across her cheek. She'd given up wearing make-up on the days she visited the cemetery. It would have needed industrial strength materials to stop it from running into tear-stained clumps.
>
> "Hey, wait. Are you O.K.?"
>
> Lisa felt her neck and back stiffen. She'd struggled through her grief very much on her own. She hated to be seen this way.
>
> "Come and sit down," said the voice, as the man *(He has*

not yet introduced himself to the viewpoint character, so we cannot at this stage know his name. If the viewpoint character does not know, then we do not know) led her towards a bench.

She flinched. He could be anyone. However, there was no real fight left in her and she followed his command.

"I'm Pete," said the stranger. "I hate coming to this place, but it's the only way to talk to Mum these days." *(The only things we can know about him are the things he tells us.)*

She looked up, shocked by the openness of someone she'd only just met. Pete's approach had seemed confident, not the type of person she imagined talking to a grave, but then she was there, so she supposed that it proved nothing. *(We can have all her impressions and thoughts as she is the viewpoint character.)*

"I was visiting my parents too," her voice faltered. "It's a year since Mum died. I've been dreading today." Her hands were trembling as she clutched the shreds of tissue. "I needed to be here at the same time she died. I don't know why."

"I didn't mean to intrude," said Pete. "Are you going to be all right? I was going to the pub when I've finished here, if you need someone to talk to who understands."

"I'm not much company at the moment," she said, wondering if it was a way of finding an excuse. "But thanks, anyway."

"Me neither. At least it would be someone to mope with. I'll be in the Red Lion if you change your mind."

She studied the even features of Pete's face, *(because she is the viewpoint character she can tell us what he looks like, but is unlikely to comment on her own appearance* except by reference to things such as her grief requiring 'industrial strength make-up')* with his gentle blue eyes and rugged chin, as he broke into a smile and Lisa began to feel better than she had done all morning.

"I'll be there about midday. It usually takes me twenty minutes to have a chat with Mum. Maybe I'll see you there." Pete smiled again, before setting off at a brisk walk *(We can learn about non-viewpoint characters from what they tell us and what they do – we see him walk briskly because Lisa sees him, the same with his smile.)* into the heart of the cemetery. She watched him go. It felt quite a surreal situation; she almost wondered whether the conversation had taken place at all.

*PC: Characters can of course see their reflection and comment on this. Please don't do that unless it's vital the reader knows how they look, as it's something of a cliché.

Multiple points of view

RJK: So far I've talked mainly about writing in a single POV in order to give the reader a close bond with your character. There can be good reason to use multiple POVs in your work, particularly in longer pieces. It is possible to write a whole novel from a single POV and many are, but you may find there are scenes you want to bring to the reader that your viewpoint character is not present for. You can use other devices such as news reports, emails, letters, phone calls and so on, to communicate the episode to them, but that might not be enough for what you want to achieve. Most of those devices will present only limited information about both what occurred and what another character thought or felt about it. At those times you might choose to use multiple POVs.

Using multiple POVs in a piece of short fiction can, if not handled carefully, be both clumsy and confusing to the reader. Your piece should contain some element of conflict or challenge. Being in the heads of the characters on both sides of a conflict can leave the reader not knowing whose side they are on. When your protagonist conquers all, the reader who feels close to the character, conquers all with them. If the reader is also being left feeling close to a defeated character, they too feel defeated and are left without the high the story could have given them. Obviously different stories follow different themes, but hopefully that illustrates the

> Being in the heads of the characters on both sides of a conflict can leave the reader not knowing whose side they are on

difficulties which can occur.

PC: Sometimes seeing the storyline from two sides can be a rewarding experience for the reader, so don't rule it out if you're sure it genuinely adds something.

RJK: In a longer work, such as a novella or novel, using multiple POVs is easier to manage and ideally they should be demarcated by a section break or separate chapter. This can work well until your viewpoint characters come together in the novel at which point handling their respective POVs can be more difficult and should at the very least be separated by a new paragraph for each. You may choose to focus much more heavily on one of those viewpoint characters, rather than try to work with them equally. Normally, one character in the novel is the lead player and they should take priority.

Modern fiction seems to favour, or at least be more accepting of, multiple POVs.

Omniscient point of view

> An omniscient narrator can see everything

Using an omniscient narrator means being able to see everything. The narrator knows all and can comment on all. The narrator can be either one of the characters in the story, or completely separate from them. Unless you are looking at the world through the eyes of God, it is the least like real life. It is worth experimenting with, but it is rarely something which writers master successfully or which readers really appreciate. Having a narrator who already knows what will happen in the future and the impact of those events on the lives and choices of the characters can be fun, but it can equally distance the reader and leave them too far from the characters themselves.

Distant or close narrative voice

The POV and narration used in third person can be very close to a character, at times giving you their inner thoughts and letting you feel what they feel, or it can be slightly looser in approach, with a more neutral impression for the reader. Different types of story will work better with different styles, and some of this you will learn through reading other work and some through practice. A crime novel from the POV of the criminal may be better kept slightly looser to prevent the reader feeling sullied and walking away. It's a little like whether it is right to use the second person in narrative. If you are writing a deeply emotional piece, then the closer you bring the reader the more they will feel the emotion.

> If you are writing a deeply emotional piece, then the closer you bring the reader the more they will feel the emotion

There can be reasons of style to keep the reader more distant. It maybe that some parts need to be close, while others have more distance. That will all come with practice and observing the impact your work has on your audience.

PC: You can go deeper into the character's POV or pull away at different points in a novel too. For example, in an emotional scene you might experience all their thoughts and feelings, even though you don't show these elsewhere. Alternatively, you can pull back from their mind to show they are distancing themselves from the action, or distracted.

Male v Female

RJK: Finally, does it matter if your protagonist is male or female and the same or opposite sex to yourself? It is a very interesting exercise to look at work in a male POV written by a woman, and in a female POV written by a man and ask yourself whether they got the voice right. In a well written piece it will be quite convincing, but...

PC: Yes, it can go horribly wrong, but we shouldn't be put off trying because of that. I often write in the POV of a man (or child, or someone who's life experience is very different from my own). If we only write about characters who're just like us, it will severely limit the number of stories we can tell.

RJK: There is not enough space here to point out all the likely pitfalls of writing the POV of a character of the opposite sex, but there are some very common mistakes. These are sweeping generalisations, and of course there are women and men who do not fit the stereotype, but the whole idea that the two sexes come from different planets is not far wrong! Here are a few as a starting point.

Colour – When you describe colour to a woman there is lemon, corn, buttercup and daffodil, to a man there is yellow! (As I've said these are generalisations and if your character is artistic, then he may of course select from a much wider palette of shades.) Your male character, if they talk about colour at all, will talk essentially about the rainbow colours and even then indigo and violet are likely to be lumped together as purple or in a worst case split between blue and red. Female characters will describe the shade of a colour as though selecting from a paint colour chart.

Communication – Women will make a phone call to hear another person's voice, to feel close to them and know they are there. They will talk about absolutely nothing and come away feeling the better for it. Men will pick up the phone when there is a fact to be conveyed and once that is done they will feel that everything necessary has been said. It is a different style.

Textures – Much like colour a man will boil down texture to the basic impact, rough, smooth, slippery and so on. A woman is more likely to feel the warp and weft of the fabric, the openness of the weave, the fineness of the silk.

> For POV to be authentic, be mindful of the voice of the opposite sex

Attitudes to weapons – There is a primeval difference between men and women. Consider the level of gun crime committed by women as opposed to men and the respective murder levels for example. Men were originally the hunters. Deep in a part of their brain is the mindset which made going out killing for food an everyday occurrence. In a modern day environment some of the instincts remain, even though the tasks have changed. Women are more likely to feel an aversion to weapons than would men.

I could carry on. None of these points is true of every woman or every man, but there are themes and patterns and if you want your POV to be authentic you need to be mindful of that as you write the voice of the opposite sex. Observation and listening to actions and conversations around you are the best ways to learn about someone most like the character you are writing. You need to get the language right for how they would speak, but you need to get the type of thing they'd talk about right too and the behaviours they would exhibit. I'm the first to argue that men and women are just as capable of achieving much the same things, but it is very important in writing to understand that, at times, they do those things in very different ways.

Although I have covered the male/female split here, the same principles can apply in writing from the POV of a different age of character, writing in a different historical period or writing from the POV of a character with a different ethnic background to give just a few examples. Keeping your voice authentic is an interesting and, when you get it right, rewarding challenge.

EXERCISE 1

Select a few pages from a favourite book, where at least two characters appear. Rewrite it from a different POV. You may find there are some parts which don't work as well, require rewording or which need you to add additional information to make them work.

EXERCISE 2

Think of an incident which has happened to you and rewrite it from the POV of someone of the opposite sex and who is much younger or older than yourself. Instead of describing how you felt and reacted, show the situation from this new character's perspective. What would they do, feel, notice and say differently?

PLOTTING

To plot or not to plot? That is the question! I'm a plotter when it comes to novels and an outliner on shorter works.

PC: I outline novels (even though I don't always stick to my own plan). Shorter pieces are rarely plotted other than in my head.

RJK: I know many people who prefer not to plot and like developments to come as much as a surprise to them as they do to the reader. Neither approach is right or wrong, it is a matter of preference, but what are the pros and cons of plotting?

The pros and cons of plotting

Which option you select will shape how much time each part of the work will take. Both can end up at a perfectly acceptable end result, but the distribution of time will look quite different. If you plot then you are likely to spend far less time rewriting, but will have a much greater up-front time commitment in preparation. If you don't plot then your editing will almost certainly be much more extensive, as you prune the dead ends that went nowhere and ensure your loose ends are tied up. If you have a clear chapter plan then the draft may not be substantially different in length to the finished work, you will still need to edit for loose ends, poorly written sections and to tighten up the flabby parts. However, if you don't plan, the chances are there will be whole sections of the draft that need to be cut, moved, or tied together.

Neither approach is right or wrong and when you are comparing with another writer how you go about things and how long each stage can take, you should bear in mind the different approaches you have each chosen. Work with the approach which best suits your style and don't be persuaded by anyone that the way you choose is wrong. In working out the way that suits you, it may be worth trying each approach to see how it feels. The only word of caution is that in not plotting you do leave yourself open to a higher likelihood of staring at a blank page for a long time, as you try to decide which direction to take the story in.

If you plot, even if you do it to the nth degree, you do need to leave room for the characters to express themselves and occasionally they may still surprise you. When this happens you need to go back and update the notes you've made on their character, their likes and dislikes and their approach to life (see character questionnaires). You may also need to rewrite your synopsis if they take you in a completely different direction

> If you plot you spend a greater time in preparation
>
> If you don't plot your editing will be more extensive

for any stage of the work. Changing your original plot, even completely, is fine. It's your story and nothing is cast in stone.

As you explore what works for you it can be fun to undertake an exercise with the same characters. Firstly, write a story where you plot nothing and just follow the grain of the idea that you have. Leave that at the first draft stage and then start again with the same characters, you may also use what you have learnt about them from your first story, and write a new story which you plot first. If you have a good writing friend it might be worth sitting down together with the two stories and discussing them in detail to see what has worked and what hasn't. You can learn a great deal by analysing your work in that way and it may help you in discovering the approach that works for you.

> There's no one right way

There is no one right way to plot. You may find if you've used the mind mapping technique outlined earlier that by extrapolating your what?, how?, why?, when?, where? questions you have enough of an outline to work with and need no further plotting, but again this may depend on the length of the work you are putting together. For a novel I start by writing out the kernel of an idea. I then start to think about the core story that it belongs to and write a first draft synopsis. What this gives me is the clear story arc (see later section). I know where my characters will start and I know where they will end up, although in my most recent book they revolted part way through and changed the ending. I then take some index cards and, by hand, write on each one a single clear event that will occur in the course of the book. This could be as simple as 'A is imprisoned for fraud', or 'B falls in love with X' and so on. I will end up with probably 30 to 50 index cards scattered around the floor. I then start to sort them into a pile with the events in some sort of order that fits with the synopsis. The chapter breaks may be as clear as one card representing a chapter, or two or three cards needing to be combined.

After that, I go back through the cards making notes of the surrounding issues that lead up to the key event noted and link it both from the previous card and to the next one. This is the point I switch to the computer and write all that as a chapter plan. Depending on what I'm writing about, that's when I would normally break off for research on all the key areas of the book. It means that the research is structured and relevant, rather than too wide ranging and can be put together broadly in the order I will need the information. That's not the end of the research as there are always things to check later, but it gives a good grounding to start to build the novel from.

Then, armed with my plan and my character questionnaires, I can begin to write the first draft and keep writing until those two glorious words 'The End'.

PC: When I started my first novel, *Paint Me A Picture*, I had no plan at all. When I'd written 80,000 words and still had no idea how it would end, I decided that approach wasn't right for me. I did finish the book, and am very happy with it, but it took ten years to get there!

I still plan in far less detail than many other authors, and do it all on the computer. I start by putting headings for each chapter (guessing how many I'll have). Under each I write the key events I intend to include. These are very much like the comments Rosemary uses on her cards. I mention which characters will appear (this helps to ensure I don't leave major protagonists out for long periods) and details such as location and time of year are included. There's usually a lot of cutting and pasting until I'm happy with the order.

At this stage I research anything which could impact on major plot events, to be sure I'm not relying on anything implausible. Then I start writing. There will be more cutting and pasting and I generally add in more plot points and characters. Anything major is added to the outline and I also use it for reminders of things I need to add or change.

EXERCISE

Before you write your next piece, write a plot outline. For a short story that could be as simple as a sentence on each of; the opening, decisive moment and ending, but include other details too if you know them already. See if it helps when writing the story.

RESEARCH

RJK: In any book, especially where you are using a different time period than the present, or are writing about any specialist area of knowledge, one of the most difficult things is to make sure your writing is authentic. It doesn't matter whether the subject is chocolate making, the workings of a hospital or the material used in clothing in the 1600s. Some writers will say, 'Does it really matter if it's fiction?' That's a fair point and, if you don't want your writing to be taken seriously then making up the bits you don't know and getting your facts wrong is a good way to achieve that. Others

> If you want your writing to be taken seriously – get your facts right!

might say, 'Does anyone really notice?' The answer to that is, most definitely, yes. Incorrect factual detail will be noted by some in their reviews and others will stop reading altogether.

Research is important in almost any work of fiction that takes you outside the realms of your own experience. If there is something you need to write about that you don't have first-hand experience of, then find out. You can ask someone who does know, give it a go yourself, if that is possible and legal, or learn about it from museums, books or lectures for example.

Even looking back to the late 1970s as I do in *The Appearance of Truth* it is very easy to misjudge how technology has changed.

Amongst the questions I found myself having to research for this book were basic ones such as 'Did Mothercare exist as a brand back then?', 'When were pay and display car parks introduced?' and 'How common, if at all, was CCTV?' They were all important considerations in the story. There were other important points that I can't tell you about for fear of spoiling the plot, but there were aspects relating to the registration of births and deaths, and child benefit.

Some research is easier to do than others and the age of the internet has brought massive time savings in looking things up. In *The Lifetracer* I needed to know what type of houses I would find on particular streets. I was using real locations and I needed there to be an alley between the houses, so I had to find locations which matched that. Nowadays, I don't need to get into the car to find out. I can simply log on to the websites Google Street View and Rightmove and I can not only see the houses, but find out how much they sell or rent for and the layout of the house both inside and out.

For *The Orphan Train* things are a little more complicated. I didn't need to know about the street layout now, but what it was in the 1800s. I needed to know which songs were written before that time and likely to be known and popular. I needed to find out about the ships crossing from Cork to New York and what the restrictions were at entry. You can still use the internet for much of that research, but be wary using Wikipedia as it is not a verified source of information and can be wrong. It is better to join some of the big libraries and use their digitised collections, or the Google Books project to get back to original reference material. Many museums have now put significant parts of their catalogues online, and don't underestimate the benefits of wading through academic papers from universities around the world.

Little can beat having first-hand experience or visiting a place you are writing about. Absorbing an atmosphere makes it much easier to produce work that draws on all the senses, but that is not always either possible or, if writing about tragedy, desirable. You will be touched and humbled by the willingness of fellow writers who have experienced tragedy to share their deepest feelings in order to help others write better fiction that covers that subject. It is one of the many reasons that belonging to a good writing community, either online or in person, can be immensely useful.

The authenticity of language is important both in regional work and in historical pieces. I read a review which dismissed Ben Elton's brilliant novel *Two Brothers* simply because it used the word teenager which was not in use in the 1930s. Most readers don't leave you for such ridiculous reasons, but it is something of which the writer needs to be aware.

If you don't check your facts and inadvertently have a mobile phone in 1967 your readers will not only notice, but stop believing the reality you have created, unless you are into time travel and science fiction and even then it is generally rooted in believable science. Good fiction writing is about helping the reader to suspend reality for the time they are in your world and taking them on a journey. If you aren't careful, getting your facts wrong is like the author coming along and melting your beautifully constructed snowman.

> If you get facts wrong, your reader will stop believing the reality you've created

EXERCISE

Take the plot outline you wrote in the previous section and imagine you are setting the story in 1925 or in a different country, such as Russia. What will you need to research to make the story authentic? How easily can you find that information using the internet and other available resources?

NAMING CHARACTERS

One of my favourite exercises when starting a new piece of writing is naming my characters. It is the point at which I breathe life into them. I've documented their age, sex, height, hair colour, employment history, schooling, likes, dislikes, pets, their fears, their hopes and dreams and now I'm going to bring them to life with a name. If I've drawn an eighteen-year-old girl and give her the name Elsie the reader's reaction is going to be an assumption the story is in the past. Very few people now call their child Elsie. Similarly, if I have someone born in 1950 in England the chance of their being called Kylie is very slim. That name only hit the UK with the Australian soap operas. It's like the name Wendy, created by J. M. Barrie. If I were to set a story earlier than 1904, to give a character the name Wendy would shout that it was not authentic for the period. Some names are safe and timeless, others go in cycles and you need to reflect, or at least not go against, the trends.

Surnames are more complex. I love the way Charles Dickens created surnames for his characters that sound plausible and yet tell you more about the character than two sentences of narration might. Sadly, I lack his genius, besides it can be overdone very easily and often does not work in serious writing. My inspiration comes from anything from the phone directory to old census records and in some instances my own family tree. Pete Laundon, the foil for my protagonist in *The Appearance of Truth*, takes his surname from one of my own distant ancestors. Sometimes I take place names and occasionally vary the spelling for good measure.

PC: If using both first and surname for a character, do carry out an online search to be sure there isn't a real person of that name who could possibly be mistaken as the inspiration for your character. It's very easy for a name to feel right because we've heard it before.

RJK: For me a name has to say something about the person.

> A name can say something about the person

Lisa Forster the protagonist in *The Appearance of Truth* is strong, but vulnerable. The first name tried to conjure this up. You can show the difference with a name like Charlotte. It's a great name but think of the difference you perceive between the rather formal Charlotte, the strong tomboy Charlie and the rather more ditzy sounding Lotti.

PC: Names can also hint at a character's ethnicity and help make them stand out in the reader's mind. Are you likely to confuse Denzil, Mark and Gupta with each other?

RJK: You can find lists of the most popular names for girls and boys in each year, on the internet. You can even find lists for other countries and some historic records. You can also find old 'Baby Name' books in many second-hand bookstores or charity shops. Do give thought to the names you give your characters and be careful, if you have favourite names, not to use the same one repeatedly. It might be as well to keep a record file of which names you've used in which story or book. If you repeat the same ones too regularly and people read a number of pieces of your work they may, mistakenly, think you have resurrected the same character and be confused when you give them an entirely different background story.

EXERCISE

You are writing a story involving a 73-year-old grandmother, her 37-year-old married daughter and her neighbours who have recently arrived into the country from Poland. What names would you give them?

TITLES

How important is a story's title? From the titles given to many submitted stories it would be easy to conclude it is an afterthought, and I am probably as guilty as the next writer of failing on this one. The title is the first thing the reader sees. It is what may make the difference to them selecting your story or selecting a different one. It needs to do two things. Most importantly it needs to hook the reader, but secondly it must reflect some key aspect of the story. For example, you might call your story 'The one that got away' but if then the theme of the story is completely different and in no way supports the idea of losing something which could have been good, then the reader may end up feeling cheated. Equally, if you simply called the story 'Fish' then it is not terribly inspiring.

> The title is the first thing the reader sees

If a short story has a title like 'Love' it builds an expectation of romance. If it turns out to be a horror story, then the reader's sensibilities may be disturbed and they may be disappointed. If a story is called 'Henry' it tells you very little about the piece and doesn't really do anything to hook you. Henry might be a bitter old man, or a small boy, he may be a dog or a vacuum cleaner. It is no indication of subject matter or quality of writing.

It's important for any story submitted, but especially with a competition entry. A story which is for publication may at least have its title changed ahead of publication. However, a competition entry has one chance to make an impression and many judges will dock marks for a poor title, I certainly do.

> Titles may attract marks in competitions

PC: When I'm judging competitions the title is often what

makes the difference between two otherwise equally good entries.

RJK: It is not just true of individual stories, but of poems and books as well. With books it's important to search on the internet to see if there are other books of the same title. If there are a number, yours may be lost among them. If the existing ones fit a genre which is very different from your own, you may find your buyers uncomfortable with the search results. It is best to do a search before you finalise your title and, if necessary, change it. It does not preclude others using that title later, but it is certainly better to make sure your book stands out.

It is easy to give pieces of work names that really don't do them justice or at the opposite extreme, try too hard. One word titles can work if the word is interesting or conjures something up in the mind of the reader, but two or three words chosen wisely can work even better. However… using the definite article (the) is going to leave your story languishing fairly low down a list that is in strict alphabetical order. Using the indefinite article (a or an) may work better for that, but again does not make the story title stand out. Lengthy titles rarely display well and tend to be cut off at some point when shown electronically, and, in my experience, are usually easily forgettable.

> Lengthy titles rarely display well

PC: Some markets have a preference for certain types or lengths of title. Choosing something which suits their page layout will make the editor's job easier and make it more likely the one you've provided will be used.

Another reason for an unusual title which reflects the story, at least as a file name, is that it will make finding that story easier in the future. If you have dozens beginning with the same word, or which are fairly meaningless, you'll need to keep opening documents to check which is which.

RJK: Beyond this, there is the question of clichés. You only have to look through the story titles on www.alfiedog.com to realise there are some which are used more often than others. If you pick the first thing that comes to mind on a particular theme, the risk is that so will many other people. If you are entering a competition you don't want your entry to have the same title as another. Avoid things like 'Valentine's Day', 'First Love' or 'Blind Date'. Choose instead something that gives a flavour of the writing and which leaves in the reader the desire to find out more.

A title should never be a throw away, given no thought whilst you focus on the story itself. See it rather as a mini story within the story. Encapsulate the heart of the story in three – five words. Making it longer than this is likely to make it ungainly and it is unlikely to be memorable. Think of book titles which make you want to know more; *A Clockwork Orange, Pride and Prejudice, Brave New World*. If you can't think of something when you start writing the story, then give it a working title and come back to it when you reach the end.

Your title may actually be the difference between your story being remembered by an editor or being forgotten and that can be the difference between selling the story or finding it languishing in the drawer!

EXERCISE

Look at a magazine you'd like to write for, a competition you'd like to win or a publisher you'd like to produce your books. Create a list of their titles. Are there any similarities? Try writing some titles yourself which would fit into the range.

BEGINNINGS

What makes you read a book or story? For most of us it is two things. We read the back cover to see a 'blurb' which gives us a flavour of the story, and we read the first page, or use the 'look inside' feature on Amazon. It is sometimes claimed that the real test is to read page 99 of a book. That page lurking in the middle of the story which still needs to be interesting. I would argue whilst that is relevant to see if it is well written and engaging, it is not a way to see if the story hooks you. If you are hooked, there are times where the story is quite legitimately slower paced, but we'll come back to that when we look at middles.

Don't start by telling me about the weather.

PC: Many classic novels do start with weather or character description. It was expected then, when the whole pace of novels was slower and they didn't have to compete with TV and Facebook to hold a reader's attention. We can't get away with it now and there's even less place for this in short stories.

RJK: How do you hook a reader at the start of the story? In general terms the key person who drives the story should be the one the reader meets first. This may not be true in all stories. For example, in a crime novel, your lead may be the detective, but you might want to start with the problem they are there to address. Opening with a dead body can be a very good hook, but it is highly unlikely, unless it's a ghost story, that they will also be your protagonist!

If you are writing in the point of view of one character they are the one who the reader needs to think and feel with throughout the book. Having said that, it is not enough to say 'Joe put on his socks as he thought through the

> Evoke a reaction in the reader

groceries he was going to need to buy.' That may well be better than the infamous 'It was a dark and stormy night.', but not much. However, it tells us little more than 1) Joe wears socks 2) he has to do some shopping. For me it has the 'so what?' element. I don't care.

It can be fun to try to evoke a reaction in the reader. I started my novel *The Lifetracer* with

> 'Who wouldn't want to investigate a death threat if given the opportunity?'

That tells the reader that there is a death threat and our lead character has the opportunity to investigate it. However, at the same time it is making the reader think 'would I want to investigate a death threat?' and brings them into the story.

It can work very well to start with speech. Take the opening of the story *A Clean Break* by Samantha Tonge:

> '"I asked for what?" Ken put down his glass of wine and skimmed a hand over his bald head.'

Here we have a good opening question. I defy anyone who reads that not to want to know what it is that Ken had actually asked for.

By starting with some action you are right into the story. In *An Unexpected Visit* Alan C. Williams starts his humorous science fiction story:

> 'As Patti Gilmore opened their front door, she was surprised to see an overweight police detective flanked by two heavily armed officers.'

Not only are you straight into the action, you know Patti is the lead character and you have a very visual image of what she is facing... and, if you are me, you are intrigued.

Although the opening sentence is important you've usually got a little longer than that to hook the reader. Sometimes it is the second sentence which provides the hook. In one of my own stories *Princess Isabella and the Tale of the Three Wishes* we are faced with an unexpected contrast that makes us take notice:

'Once upon a time, there was a beautiful princess. She had buck teeth and thick-lensed glasses, but she was a beautiful princess none-the-less.'

You have no more than about 50 words to make the reader interested. On www.alfiedog.com we include the opening lines of the story, as well as the blurb, for the reader to get a feel before they download a story. It is worth reading a few and deciding what works for you and what doesn't. You can select stories in a particular genre to get the closest comparison to your own writing. (The above stories are all taken from the site.)

> You have around 50 words to hook your reader

A good opening is important in both short stories and novels. Lee Child's novel *Without Fail* gives a perfect study in how to hook your reader:

> A good opening is important

'They found out about him in July and stayed angry all through August. They tried to kill him in September. It was way too soon.'

To me that is a great opening. Who did they find out about? Why did it make them angry? Who was he? Why didn't their attempt to kill him work? And of course, the follow on – How are they going to make sure it works next time?

The style is simple and effective. There is no wasted description, but it sets the scene for a crime novel. We know there will be a killing. We know it is autumn. We know that for whatever reason he only came to their attention in July. It makes you want to read on.

Remember the rest of the story must live up to the opening. If it's a gentle love story, then a really dramatic opening might not be appropriate and you'll need to hook the reader another way. Different genres will require different styles and different subjects for the hook, but it doesn't matter whether you need to start with:

'As he leaned forward her scent caught him off guard and his pulse quickened.'

Or

'Being born with eight arms was thought by most to be useful, but finding the right armhole of his spacesuit was close to impossible.'

Whatever your genre, you need to hook your reader at the beginning of your story. This is not the place to set out the backstory of your characters and all the events leading up to the action. Better to start with the action and get the reader interested. Even then, only bring in backstory in snippets as it is directly relevant, don't feel the need to give a whole chunk of explanation.

Your opening is your chance to make an impression on the reader. Use it wisely or the reader will move on to the next book or story and yours will be ignored.

EXERCISE

Read some story openings (they're free to access) on www.alfiedog.com, or in an anthology or magazine, (choose ones in different genres). Do they help you decide whether the story appeals to you or not? What encourages you to read on, or puts you off?

Now select one of the titles you created in the exercise on titles and write an opening paragraph to go with it. If it's gripping enough perhaps you'll want to write on and find out what happens.

DIFFERENT GENRES

The principles of good writing are broadly similar whoever your intended reader, but some are worth noting for specific genres.

Genre fiction is all fiction which can be pigeon-holed into subjects such as 'romance', 'crime', 'science fiction', 'horror' etc. There are categories for every type of book, but some are easier to categorise than others. New genres appear at intervals. Some of those are very helpful and others seem to confuse the choices. My comments below relate to some of the higher level genres, but are applicable to the sub-divisions below them.

Many writers choose to specialise in one particular genre and the choice is often driven by what they enjoy reading. There are good writers in all genres, but below I have set out some of the more common problems I see when editing.

> Horror stories need emotional drive to scare anyone

Writing a horror story which lacks emotional drive is not going to scare anyone. Gruesome and repulsive is not a substitute for leaving the reader with a faster heart rate and jumping at the slightest noise. However much blood and gore you write into the scene is not what makes something scary. What will really unnerve the reader is the atmosphere that you build; the dark, the quiet, the expectation that something is there and they don't know what it is. If you can build the atmosphere then the reader will be breathing heavily, listening intently, feeling their heart racing as if they need to be ready for their own fight or flight response. If you do none of that but simply say 'There was a severed limb, three pints of blood and the index finger of the other hand', then whilst it's mildly unpleasant it is not going to stop the reader sleeping.

In science fiction 'showing' rather than 'telling' often seems to be forgotten. Of course you need to relay to the reader that your creature has four arms, but it is far more effective to show them multi-tasking than tell the reader how many limbs are involved. Equally, emotion will bring a science fiction story to life and have the reader caring about your aliens, or your alternate world. If you've read any Terry Pratchett you are likely to have met one of my favourite characters… Death. He's not an obvious character to root for, but the way Terry Pratchett demonstrates Death's bemusement at the world, and portrays his softer side, creates a wonderfully three dimensional and often amusing character.

In romance, the whole story will hang on emotion, but that doesn't mean you can leave aside properly managing point of view, or your research to give the story some depth. Try reading Sue Moorcroft's *Want to Know a Secret* which is an excellent example of a book with quality research. It shows in every detail, from the helicopter, to the clothes designing of the lead character and the motivation for self-harm of one of the teenagers.

Research is relevant for every story or book, but perhaps most of all in historical fiction. It is important, even writing about the relatively recent past, to get your use of technology right and not give an iPhone to someone in a story set in 1980. If you are writing historical fiction the other major problem is ensuring that the language you use is relevant to the period. If in doubt, find another word or expression that would have been in use. Research can usually reveal how long a word has been around.

There are stylistic differences between genres too. A crime novel may well have shorter sentences, and short chapters as a way to build and maintain suspense. By contrast a more literary piece may have sentences which are poetic and rather longer.

Children's literature will have sentence structures and words suitable for the reader's age. Of course it is all right to include some words that will challenge their reading, but it you use too many the story will be hard to follow and be set aside in favour of another.

Fiction should be well written whatever genre it is in. All writers need to learn their craft. There are few to whom it

> All fiction should be well written

comes completely naturally. Characters need to be developed and well rounded, research needs to be thorough and a subject factually correct, and a story needs to have emotion and feed all of the reader's senses. A good story does all these things whereas a bad one lies flat on the page.

> ## EXERCISE
>
> Choose a story in a different genre to your usual reading and writing. Note down how the style of writing differs. Where does the focus lie and do you think the writer has created the right atmosphere for the genre of the story?

SECTION 3

HOW TO WRITE

WHAT YOU'LL NEED ONCE YOU'VE GOT GOING

Notebooks

PC: Even if, like me, you prefer to write straight onto a computer, it's sensible to have a notebook too. Most likely you'll acquire far more than any non-writer would consider sensible. They can be hard to resist. My advice is not to try. I further advise that a few weeks prior to your birthday and any other occasion where people might wish to buy you gifts, repeatedly utter the phrase 'a writer can never have too many notebooks'.

If you'd rather do most of your initial writing by hand then you'll need lots of easy to use, inexpensive notebooks for general writing.

You'll need smallish ones to carry around with you and perhaps separate ones for research notes, plotting, record keeping and to do lists. Remember they're for writing in. Don't buy any which are too nice to use, or you feel should be kept for really good or important writing. If they don't encourage you to pour out every idea in your head, then they're a hindrance and not a help.

Computer

Almost all writers will use a desktop computer, laptop or tablet for some stages of their work. I use a laptop for everything from note taking and first drafts to the submission of the finished piece. I take it with me almost everywhere I go. Others only transfer finished work onto their computer so that it can be emailed, or printed out. The best method for you is the one you prefer.

You will need to use a computer to submit work. Very few places will consider hand-written submissions.

Any computer will do the job. If it doesn't come with word

processing software you can either buy Microsoft Word, or download Open Office (free but donations welcome) or one of the other alternatives, or use a specialist writing package such as Scrivener. Don't be talked into upgrades and extra features unless you need them for something else. A whole novel uses less space than one high resolution photo, so if yours is running slowly it's unlikely to be due to your writing.

The computer you already have, or a friend's discarded old one is ideal. Don't buy anything new, including more software, until you've completed a few writing projects and know what will best suit your needs. It takes a while to adapt to a new machine, so it's a waste of valuable writing time to keep changing, even if you can afford to do that.

RJK: If you are going to use it to connect to the internet, do think of suitable virus protection. No one wants a document submitted to them which contains a virus.

Printer

PC: Depending on what you intend to do with your writing, you might need to use a printer. If you'll rarely print out work then perhaps your boss or a friend will allow you to use theirs, or it might be possible to do it in the library or an office supply shop.

If you do decide to buy one, take into account the cost of replacement inks as well as the price of the machine. Again you don't want anything fancy. As long as it can print easily readable type in black ink, it's perfect.

Back-up system

You must back-up or keep copies of all work! Computers crash, bags get stolen or lost, documents can be accidentally

> Back-up or keep copies of all work

deleted... There are far too many ways the stories you've spent days or years perfecting can be lost forever.

Thankfully there are plenty of ways to ensure this doesn't happen. You could print out all your finished work and leave it with a friend. Stories can be emailed to yourself or uploaded to a website or blog (but not made publicly visible). You can place them in the Cloud, using products such as OneDrive, Box or Dropbox.

Work can be downloaded onto an external storage device such as a flash drive or hard disk.

Personally I have two hard drives. One is kept at home and one in the campervan.

RJK: I use Cloud storage so that everything I do whilst online is backed up without any further thought. It also retains previous copies of documents, so if I make a silly mistake and unintentionally overwrite something, I can still get back to the original version. If I work offline, then it backs up as soon as I connect. It also means I can access my work from an internet café or friend's computer if for any reason mine is not available, and even from my phone.

PC: I'm away in the campervan so often that I need to be able to work offline for extended periods. If I had more consistent internet access, I'd be tempted by this method too.

Writing space

A spacious office would be nice. Or even a corner of a quiet room set aside as a dedicated writing area. If you can do this, and find you write there for long periods, then try to get a properly supportive chair and arrange things so your head and arms are in a comfortable position. Ensure the lighting is adequate and if possible that the temperature is comfortable.

Don't fall into the trap of thinking you must always be in the 'right' place to work. Being comfortable and having everything you might need to hand is ideal, but don't waste writing opportunities just because you're away from your desk. Take a laptop or notebook with you everywhere and write wherever you go.

> Write wherever you go

RJK: I've even been known to dictate into my mobile phone while out walking one of the dogs.

Freedom from distractions

PC: For most of us this isn't possible over extended periods. Could you switch off the phone and internet and ask to be left alone for just half an hour so you can get started? Once you're properly involved in your story you won't notice much else anyway.

Would ear plugs or headphones help? Could you sit in the car or shed, go to the library, get to work early or stay late and write there?

How about setting aside a period each week as your writing time and letting everyone know you're not available then?

> Set aside a specific time each week

Your family, friends, pets, work and other commitments are all important, so are you and the things you wish to achieve. You are just as entitled to write as others are to be given a lift to a friend's house, have you listen to their problems, be reminded where you put their clean clothes or how to find the kitchen...

Time

There's no getting away from it, writing uses up time and most of us don't have enough. There's a section in this book on finding and using it, but don't think you need enough time to write a novel. No one has that, especially not novelists. You need enough time to write some of your story; even a few words each day add up.

RJK: If you are going to snatch time, it might be worth setting an alarm for when you need to finish. It is all too easy to get engrossed and miss your next appointment!

Classes and workshops

PC: Do take some of these if you possibly can. They're valuable for learning new skills and improving existing ones, but good ones do much more than this. Often they'll be extremely motivating, will encourage you to try something new and provide some feedback. Usually they're fun. There are general writing classes for people of all experience levels and for specific genres or types of writing, so you should be able to find something to suit your needs.

If you can't physically attend a course, there are some very good ones online, or conducted by post.

Writing groups

Writers need to be in contact with other writers. We must have feedback, encouragement and support from those who understand the process. A good writing group will provide all this. There may also be talks, competitions, exercises and cake.

> Writers need to be in contact with other writers

A bad group, or one which doesn't suit your current needs, can be demoralising. Different groups focus on different things. Some might simply read and critique each other's work, others will discuss various aspects of writing or may be more of a social and support network.

Writing groups may meet physically or online. Try several and only persevere with those which are genuinely of help and interest to you. If you can't find what you want, then start your own.

Magazines and books

There are a lot of publications which are potentially useful to writers. *Writing Magazine* and *Writers' Forum* both provide interesting articles, market news and competitions. The *Writers' & Artists' Yearbook* is a brilliant resource if you are hoping to find a publisher or agent. There are also many books on different aspects of the craft of writing.

It's easy to get carried away and spend so much time reading about writing that you have none left in which to put theory into practice. You'll also need to read any publications you wish to submit to, but although all these can be valuable, don't get too many at once.

Internet presence

If you intend to either self-publish any work, or submit books to a publisher you'll need to promote and market these and to do that effectively you need a strong internet presence. It takes time to get to grips with the technology and far longer to gain followers, so if you expect to need this in the future, start now.

The internet is also useful for finding information, support and encouragement, and is a brilliant research tool for public opinion. What it's absolutely best at is wasting our time! Although I strongly suggest you have at least one social media account (Twitter, Facebook, Pinterest etc.) and a blog or website if you'll need to promote your work, please don't try to be everywhere, and do your best to restrict the time you spend online.

Qualifications

If you'd like to study for a qualification in writing and have the time and money to do so, you might well find it a rewarding experience. If you'd rather not, or don't have the resources then not to worry. Having a creative writing degree, or any other qualification won't in itself make your writing better (although what you learn certainly might) nor will it make it any easier to get published. Publishers, editors and readers care about the words in front of them, not the letters after the author's name.

If you intend to teach writing, then a qualification will be an advantage, but even then your experience and publishing credits will generally be considered more valuable.

Ideas

You'll need lots of ideas. That's what writing is; expressing ideas. Luckily they're everywhere, loads of them. Lots and lots are already in your head just waiting for you to notice, but if you're finding it difficult to recognise them see the relevant sections of this book to get you started.

Persistence

You'll need bucketloads of persistence both to improve as a writer and to keep editing your work until it's as good as you can make it. If you hope for publication, you'll need even more for that.

Skills

There are a number of skills required to write well. You'll need to grasp punctuation and grammar, be able to structure your work, use dialogue, bring characters to life, engage the reader, handle tenses and point of view, add conflict, edit... Once you are writing work worth reading, you'll have to learn how to format it, how and where to send it, how to keep track of your work, what to do about any payments you receive... Don't worry, you can learn as you go and we're here to help.

THE MIDDLE

RJK: However good your opening is, if the middle does not sustain the story momentum then you will not produce a good read.

There are many things I tell writers not to do in the opening of the story – don't include too much backstory, don't start with description rather than action and so on. None of that means you can simply shunt those into the middle of the story. The middle should be where the characters rise to the challenge they are facing, hunt the dragon they are to slay, come face to face with the enemy in whatever form it takes.

If you find yourself slipping into a chunk of backstory you most likely need to ask yourself two questions: 'How relevant is it to the story as a whole?' and, 'Have I started the story in the right place?' If you are drawn to spend the whole of the middle of the story in the past, I would strongly urge you to look at whether you've picked the wrong starting point. Ask yourself 'What is the point of my story?' and then stick to it. I am by nature an inveterate planner. I can't help myself and what I am about to say may be seen as a bias as a result of that, however, I think those at the biggest risk of finding the middle of the story sagging are those writers who claim they like their story to be free flowing and prefer not to plan. When you do this it is far easier to forget the point of the story. You might have in your head the opening and the end point and think your characters will wend their way from one to the other without guidance. If you are lucky this will be the case, but not all characters are that efficient and some will lead you off at a tangent to the story. In the same way there are loquacious individuals who will ramble on amiably without getting to the point, some of your characters will do this as well and, pleasant as they are, they do

> Keep in mind the point of the story

not make for the best story-tellers.

PC: Yes, Rosemary is biased in favour of planning, but she's also right about this. Without a plan it's very easy to either get sidetracked to the detriment of the main storyline, or write long sections where not very much happens. You can edit that out later, but try to guard against doing it in the first place.

RJK: In a longer piece, the pace of the middle of the story needs to vary. If you are writing action, your reader will become worn out if the pace stays at full speed for too long. It needs to alternate with quieter times to allow them to catch their breath before the next adventure. By contrast if you are writing a slow paced piece, if it is too slow for too long you will lose your reader to sleep.

In short, make your middle count. Make sure it serves a purpose and propels the story forward and that the pace is one the reader can enjoy. Use it to set up the finale, but

> Make your middle count

without giving the ending away. This is where the conflict in the story will come in. Set up the challenge that your protagonist has to overcome, lay the clues out that your detective needs to follow, build the story that will lead to your twist ending. The middle of your story is vital.

EXERCISE

Go back to the plot you sketched out earlier; write a couple of sentences on what action and events will sustain the middle of the story.

CONFLICT

Stories are rarely satisfying if they contain no challenge or if the overcoming of the challenge is not brought about by the protagonist's own actions. If everything in a story is too easy, the reader gets to the end and says, 'So what?' If the overcoming of the challenge is 'the fairy waved her magic wand' and no one had to do anything, then the reader feels cheated. You want your reader to be rooting for your hero or heroine, holding their breath when they think the character won't make it, letting out a long sigh when they overcome the hurdle and gasping with horror as they see the next challenge looming ahead.

All stories need conflict

Conflict or challenge can come in many ways. It can be opposition imposed by other individuals in the story (bereavement, divorce, argument), it can be an external situation which arises such as redundancy, war, flooding, earthquake etc. or it can be a character's own internal struggle against demons, maybe overcoming a phobia or facing up to events from the past. It can also be the protagonist having to deal with serious illness or injury.

The key in a longer piece of fiction is to build up the situation of challenge and keep building it until it looks as though the character can't possibly take any more, then help them to take steps forward. When they start to find a way through the problem, pile on the pressure again until it appears unbearable. In a short story a single conflict is generally enough. Those conflicts don't have to be big or serious. As long as the reader sees the character cares about the situation, then they are likely to care as well.

Eventually, have your character take natural steps to overcome the challenge, but not to do so easily. The end result must be a product of the story. The overcoming should not be out of the blue or by a sudden twist. Winning the lottery is not a satisfying solution to someone's debt worries and potential homelessness, nor is a distant, previously unmentioned relative leaving them a large sum of money. Maybe occasionally those things do happen in real life, but they aren't going to work for the reader in fiction.

In *The Appearance of Truth* my heroine is on her way to meet someone who may be able to tell her the truth of her birth. Her boyfriend insists on driving, so she is no longer in control of the situation. His car breaks down in the middle of nowhere. There is no mobile phone signal. She walks off in the direction they were going in search of a phone. When she finds one, the taxi company don't turn up and so it continues.

When you are writing a story and you think it can't get any worse, then as the writer, remember to tighten the screws some more! Squeeze every ounce of stress and suspense out of the situation before your hero or heroine comes through in the end. This is true of any length of story. Obviously there is room for fewer twists and turns in a short story, but there must still be enough challenge to make the story worth reading.

EXERCISE 1

Using the story plot you have been developing, what conflict will occur in the story and how will it be overcome?

EXERCISE 2

Put a character in a difficult situation. Have them begin to resolve the problem and then make things even worse for them.

EDITING FOR STORY LENGTH

PC: If we're writing only for ourselves, stories can be any length we like. Any which seem to drag, or have become over complicated can be tightened up. If we've rushed some sections, or failed to show an important point, we can go back and add it in. No problem.

When we're writing with the intention of submitting the piece for publication, or entering into a competition, we often have a word count to comply with. It may be very precise; some flash fiction competitions won't allow a single word over or under a certain figure. More often you'll be allowed some leeway. If the guidelines state 'about' or 'approximately' you might get away with being up to 10% out. Do get as close as you can without spoiling the story. The figures will have been given for a reason.

> If a word count is given as 'approximately' work within a 10% tolerance

RJK: If a requirement gives a maximum or a minimum word count assume they are rigid. Count only the words in the story, usually excluding the title, unless it says otherwise. Submitting a minimum word count that only gets to that number because you've included your name and address in the figures is not the way to get your writing considered.

If the story is too long

PC: Can you reduce the number of characters, or simplify a storyline? Cut any description which isn't vital to the plot and the same goes for any scenes which don't move the story on. Beginners often 'write themselves in' to a story, or continue adding words once the plot has been resolved. Start as late, and finish as early, as you dare. (Do this even when you're not attempting to reduce the word count.)

You should already have eliminated any unnecessary words, but check again. Some, that, very, had, though, are all words which can often be cut. Have you been heavy handed with adjectives or modifiers? Check your dialogue. All the 'hello, how are you?' stuff can go. Do you really need all those speech tags?

RJK: Use stronger verbs and drop the adverbs.

PC: Have you used lots of words to show a minor point, which could be told much more succinctly? Yes, showing is generally better, but telling is a lesser crime than having your work disqualified for going over the allowed word count.

Be precise. There aren't 'at least a couple of dozen' cows in the field, there are 25. Check for unintentional repetitions or excessive detail.

Cut in stages. I suggest cutting and pasting it somewhere else; it's easier to be brave if you can change your mind. First cut everything you don't need, then tighten up everything you do. I'm certain the result will be at least as good as the original, if not better.

If the story is too short

This is a trickier problem to resolve. If you simply do the opposite of the above suggestions, you'll have a story with unnecessary scenes, descriptions and characters. Adding words, rather than telling more of the story, is padding. Don't do it.

> Adding words, rather than telling more of the story, is padding

Showing, rather than telling is one of the few ways to increase the word count as well as improve the story. Even this can be overdone, so be sure the point warrants the space you allocate to it.

The key is to add value and interest. You may be able to introduce a subplot, put more obstacles in the hero's way, make use of the senses or add a few descriptive details to bring characters or scenes to life. If you decide to increase the number of characters, be sure to give them a definite role.

Remember that any changes made must be woven throughout the story and become an important part of the whole.

If that's not enough

It's almost always possible to reduce the length of a story, but there's a risk that in doing so you'll lose your writing style and end up with a bland summary of events. It's difficult to increase a story's length without adding unnecessary words and therefore weakening the shorter version. Often it will be better to find an alternative home for that piece and create something fresh which fits the required word count.

EXERCISE 1

Here's a 190 word story – can you cut it without weakening it? (You're allowed to tweak the punctuation.)

Afternoon Tea

Agatha is very old and she lives all on her own now she's a widow. She's feeling a little bit thirsty so she decides she'll have a nice cup of tea.

Agatha slowly and carefully pours warm and fragrant tea into the little dainty, delicate cup. After adding about 50 ml of semi-skimmed, pasteurised milk and a little bit of white granulated sugar. Two milk chocolate digestive biscuits are precariously balanced on the matching saucer. Carefully she carries her treat into the living room.

Her favourite piece of music which is a symphony by Austrian composer Mozart plays on the modern electrically powered stereo device. She sits down on an upholstered armchair. It's the sort of shade of fresh blue the sky goes after a storm and very comfortable. She gets herself settled and a quiet contented sigh escapes her thin pink lips.

You wouldn't know it from looking at her but it's the last breath she'll ever breath out. The tea she took such trouble to make and had been looking forward to cools and is completely untasted. The biscuits aren't eaten either. She's dead which is very sad.

I'm sure that even without trying very hard you spotted a few words which could be cut and that your new version is better than the longer one.

I managed to get it down to 33.

Afternoon Tea

Agatha pours tea into the cup, adding milk. Two biscuits are balanced on the saucer. She carries her treat into the living room. A final sigh escapes her lips. The tea cools untasted.

That's a drastic cut, but all the important details are still there.

EXERCISE 2

Now try adding to the word count. You can either add in your own details or reinstate some of those I've just removed.

Here's my final version:

Afternoon Tea

Agatha pours fragrant tea into the delicate cup. After adding milk and a little sugar, two chocolate biscuits are balanced on the saucer. Carefully she carries her treat into the living room. Her favourite symphony plays on the stereo. She sits and a contented sigh escapes her lips. It's the last breath she'll ever exhale. The tea cools untasted.

It's 59 words and I bet you a cream cake you think it's better than the long-winded one. I hope you agree that I haven't simply added words to the shortest version, but also a little value and interest.

EXERCISE 3

RJK: A writing group I'm part of did something similar as an exercise. One person wrote, the next cut, the next extended. It is very interesting to see what another makes of a story in this way. Why not try teaming up with a writing buddy and seeing what they could cut a piece of your work down to, without losing the story, and do the same for them. Then do the other way round and extend a piece.

SPOKEN WORD V WRITTEN WORD

RJK: Formal written English is not always easy to read aloud. There's a reason for that. The style of writing of the written word and the spoken word are often quite different. In formal writing it is normal to write words in full without using contractions. If you do that in speech it will sound stilted and at times plain wrong. In fiction the level of formality may vary a little with the style of the writing, but rarely approaches that of a formal report in something like the Financial Times. The more you practice your writing, the more you will find your own style. You only have to read the different sections of this book to see that Patsy and I each have a style of our own. Whatever your style, there are a few points worth bearing in mind.

If you plan to have your work recorded as an audio book, or use it at a public reading, then make sure it flows for being read aloud. You may often have to reorder sentences, or iron out trip hazards to ensure that when you come to read it to an audience you can do so without struggling.

Use natural speech patterns

Use natural speech patterns, particularly in dialogue and first person narration. People do not speak in complete, grammatically correct sentences. Similarly, first person narration needs to be true to the character narrating, in terms of the voice which is used. It's all about keeping the writing authentic. You might have a scene where Joe has to call Kelly to come in from the garden for dinner. To some extent the nature of the speech is going to depend on the degree of familiarity, ages and relationship between the two characters.

Joe is the butler: "Excuse me, Madam, your dinner is served."
Joe is Kelly's brother: "Hey, sis, grub's up."
Joe is a parent: "Kelly, dinner's ready."

Only the first, very formal call, uses no contraction of speech. If you were to do that with either of the others, then they would not seem natural. People rarely speak in precise and correct terms. Very often they don't speak in complete sentences at all.

"What are you thinking?"
"Nothing."
"You can't be not thinking."
"Can, so."
"Can, not!"
"It's easy."

In this brief dialogue the characters are speaking naturally with contraction and without regard for sentence construction. Of course you still have to punctuate it in a manner which enables the reader to understand and will want to use appropriate tags so they know who is speaking.

One of the best ways to see how natural your writing is, is to read it aloud, ideally to someone else. You are more likely to stumble over the bits that are clumsy than reading silently when more often the brain simply corrects what is there as you go along. Reading it to someone else will also give the opportunity to see if it is as clear to a third party as it is to you. If your meaning is not clear, that is not because the third party is in some way inferior, it is because you – the writer – have not communicated your meaning well enough and you need to go back to rewrite.

In speech phrases like 'it is', 'that is', 'how is' 'what is', 'they had', 'they would' and many more are rarely said in their entirety. Is, had, would, have, am, will, are, not – are all commonly shortened in speech and in narrative which is less formal and in keeping with the narrative voice. Don't be afraid to make your writing natural. It will also make it more approachable.

However, and there's always a 'but', be careful not to slip into colloquial expressions and phrases, or to write in your local dialect, unless doing so deliberately. Whilst that can lead to interesting writing in its own genre, it

> Beware of colloquial expressions

does not make it easy for widespread reading. If you are making one of your characters speak in dialect, it is often better to use sparing touches to hint at it and give the reader that impression than to try to write something which can be incomprehensible to the reader. Never underestimate the number of 'local' words you use. When I opened up my latest novel to early readers I was questioned on the word 'puthered', as in 'The smoke puthered back across the train.' I explained, what to me is a very normal and meaningful word. I drew a blank. When I looked it up I was staggered to find I had managed to get through over fifty years without even realising that one was regional.

PC: I do the same with naval slang. Although I didn't grow up with 'Jackspeak', I'm now so used to it, being married to an ex matelot and having worked with the mob, I forget not everyone will have a Scooby when I tell them to pull up a bollard so I can spin them a dit.

RJK: The language you use, however formal or informal, needs to be appropriate for the piece and style you are writing.

EXERCISE

Read your latest piece of writing out loud. Keep a pen in your hand and note anywhere you stumble, feel the need to add, contract or omit words and rewrite appropriately.

THE PSYCHOLOGY OF WORD CHOICE

The English language is a magical tool. You can create emotion, atmosphere, and a very clear train of thought according to the words you use. Your choice of words will directly affect your reader, but you need to understand the impact will not be the same for every person.

> The English language is a magical tool

Let's take gender as an example. Leaving aside the question of readers more often picking up work by their own sex, your word choice will also have a bearing. Take as an example a job advert. A company does not need to say 'we want a woman' or 'we want a man' to do this job, of course that would be illegal, but they can achieve the same aim by the language they use in the advert. If you have a position that is for a period of twelve months and you say it is 'maternity cover' you conjure the image that it is a job done by a woman at present, as a result very few men will apply. If you say it is a 'twelve month fixed term contract' you take away the illusion of it being a 'woman's job' and the balance of applicants will change. Once you start to understand the background to this, you can use it in many ways. The words dynamic, ambitious, high-achieving, leader – will ensure the position attracts more male candidates, whereas – liaison, co-ordinator, customer-focussed are likely to attract proportionately more women. Now think about that in the context of your writing and move away from the field of sex discrimination.

Your reader will react to your writing as a direct result of the words you choose. That can mean you conjure emotion, call them to action, or leave them reading something else. Every word a reader hears comes not with a neutral dictionary definition but with a lifetime of usage and perceptions.

'He strode across the room and smacked his hand on the table. "Who is with me?"'

Even without further description you start to picture a large man, facing a conflict situation and wanting to know who is on his side in the fight.

'He tiptoed across the room and laid his hand on the table. "Who is with me?"'

You have exactly the same dialogue as before. You have a male character and yet, instead of a warrior you hear a diffident man who is worrying there might be someone else there.

Fundamentally in the above two examples you have used the same meaning but what you have conveyed is completely different.

I only have to think about how arguments start in my own home to know how the accidental choice of emotive language can make a situation flare up. You need to be conscious of this in your writing and use it to good effect. A 'misplaced' word in a conversation between your characters can easily be used to create a misunderstanding. It can also be used very effectively in humorous writing, with misunderstandings leading to comical situations.

> Writers need to manipulate readers' reactions

It is up to the writer to manipulate the reader's reactions. If you are writing a bad guy then you don't want the reader to like them. This filters through into every aspect of your writing. Don't describe the smartly dressed baddy as 'dapper' describe him as 'sharply dressed'. Dapper is too friendly a word to create a negative image. If I say 'handsome' rather than 'beautiful' most people think something masculine is being described. If I use the word 'little' it tends to be associated with lamb, girl and other links that show less maturity. Small is often more comfortable in an adult context.

It is all right for an author to use words which make the reader reach for the dictionary, as long as it really is the best word to express what you mean, but if you leave them doing that every sentence they will lose the flow of the story. If you have a very wide vocabulary, showing it off in your writing does not make you look clever, it makes you look pretentious. If that is what you want, then fine, but don't be surprised when you have few readers and poor reviews from others. Choosing over-clever, flowery language does not equal literary fiction. Good writing which is beautiful and poetic might achieve that. If you try too hard then the risk is that you write a piece which will be described as 'over-written' and does not make good reading.

Sentence construction is important as well. Short words, in short sentences will make the book faster paced. Longer words in meandering sentences will slow it down. Style is important and needs to match the genre and impact you are looking for.

> Sentence construction is important

PC: The meaning of words can change too. Slang terms quickly become dated. Some words used innocently in the past now have sexual implications, and many words once routinely used to describe people from different ethnic backgrounds, or with disabilities are no longer considered acceptable. Be aware that when written, offensive terms and swear words often seem much stronger.

Who we, or the characters, are speaking to also makes a big difference. Our word choices may well be different when addressing friends, those we dislike, our boss, someone we're trying to impress...

RJK: Words have life of their own. Which ones you choose and how you combine them is the ultimate power a writer can wield. Use them wisely and be conscious of their potential impact.

EXERCISE

Try having a character issue an invitation to another, but make it clear they don't really want their offer to be accepted.

STEREOTYPES

PC: Imagine your company is advertising two jobs; bricklayer and receptionist. A pretty, blonde girl in a tight skirt and a fit looking, tanned young man in jeans and a check shirt both ask for application forms. Would you ask which one they each wanted? Probably not – even if you're fully convinced women are perfectly capable of laying bricks.

In real life stereotypes are often a bad thing. They stop us seeing people as individuals and can lead to discrimination. People think they know what a mugger or terrorist looks like. They believe they can recognise a respectable law abiding individual when he's standing, in his smart suit with a charming smile, right before them. These stereotypes are very often wrong. We know this, but even so, we can't help judging people according to them. This can be very helpful to writers but it can also be a hindrance.

You can surprise the reader a little by making your flame-haired beauty shy and very slow to show her annoyance, or by having a male nurse assisting your female dentist or doctor. Readers like to be surprised as long you don't trick them or add something so unexpected it makes no sense. Stereotypes can help misdirect your reader in a twist ending story. We'll assume the person trying to get dinner ready, change 'our Billy's' nappy and do the ironing is Billy's mother – but of course they could be the father, a grandparent or sibling.

Stereotypes can be used as a form of shorthand for minor characters. We can refer to a policeman, vicar, stock broker, bottle blonde or homeless person and the reader will fill in their own physical description and probably make a few assumptions with regard to personality. With just one word or phrase, we'll have created someone who seems real.

RJK: However, as with clichés if you fill your work with perceived stereotypes you will end up with a story that is two-

> If you fill your work with stereotypes your story will lack depth

dimensional. If by contrast you fill it with either extreme versions of those stereotypes or the complete opposites of what is expected then it might work if you are writing humour, but is unlikely in any other genre. You need to use them judiciously.

You need to look beyond stereotyping to the personality types that are drawn to particular occupations because they are a good fit. Play on the strengths and weaknesses of the character type to draw out conflict. Rather than just working with classic stereotypes look a little deeper. The mousy, quiet, but ordered persona drawn to be a librarian is often there because she or he is more comfortable in that situation. If you give him a role as a telephone-sales executive, then he is likely to have a breakdown within weeks of being put under pressure to perform. That might give you a completely different story. If you start by constructing your characters, then you can decide whether to put them in situations they are comfortable in or challenge them to try something new.

Some of this will depend what market you are writing for. Make sure you know the market and what is expected before you construct your characters.

EXERCISE

Create a character who seems to fit an established stereotype, except for in one significant way. Have another character realise and react to this difference.

SHOW V TELL

Showing and telling both have a place in your writing. If you show every detail, your writing can become a long-winded way to impart something which could have been told in five words. However, too much telling will leave your work feeling like a newspaper report and lacking in life and depth to your reader. Many writers find understanding the difference between these two difficult, so it's best use examples.

> Showing and telling both have a place in your writing

You have a character about to enter the room. There are many many ways you can say that.

'Joe walked into the room. He was angry.'

Here you have told the facts in as uninteresting a way as possible. Admittedly it only took eight words but the reader has had no more than the basic actions and state of the character conveyed to them. This is telling.

'Joe stamped into the room, his face a livid red.'

Once again Joe is angry but you get to see it rather than be told it. It is more as though you are in the room and see him for yourself.

You might show Joe entering the room in other ways. Bear in mind the previous section on the psychology of words and think about the different impressions the word choices create.

'Joe swaggered into the room, whistling *I did it my way.*'

Here you get the impression that Joe is feeling self-satisfied about something and is quite relaxed and maybe more than a little arrogant.

> 'Joe opened the door a few inches and peered around the edge, his eyes darting from side to side.'

Here Joe is obviously nervous of entering, although at this stage we don't know why.

I could continue bringing Joe into the room in many ways to create a different impression. Instead let's turn to something Jane might say. Again you will see the psychology of language coming in as well as the difference between showing and telling.

Jane is about to apologise to Ruth for ruining the dress she borrowed from her.

Telling would be very basic:

> 'Jane said to Ruth that she was sorry for spilling red wine down the dress she had borrowed from her.'

Telling uses fewer words

You have reported what was said rather than showing the dialogue and whilst you have accurately reflected the situation we have seen none of the demeanour of the characters or how they are feeling about the incident.

If you are showing, then you open up more possibilities:

> "Oh I'm sorry I spilt red wine down your damn dress, but if Peter hadn't been so bloody stupid it would never have happened."

What do we take from this? Jane is not really sorry. She is casting the blame elsewhere and her apology is at best superficial.

> "Ruth, I'm so very sorry. I really didn't mean to and I'm more than happy to replace the dress. I hope it didn't have sentimental value."

Here Jane is sorry and has immediately offered recompense.

In the first one the word 'damn' in the initial part of the sentence completely changes the emphasis. 'I'm sorry I spilt wine down your dress' is a neutral statement. In itself and without what

> One word can change the whole context

follows it is unlikely to inflame the recipient, unless it was accompanied by antagonistic body language. However, add the word 'damn' and immediately Ruth is going to go on the defensive as Jane is on the attack. It's only one word, but it can change the whole context of the comment.

Equally, a character addressing a room of people might say "I'm fed up with how things are." It's a neutral statement. It might give rise to discussion, but it's not going to change the world. It's simply telling a piece of information. However, if that same character were to say. "How many of you feel you have been short-changed by the management? How many of you feel you have been asked to work too many hours? How many of you need to take home more pay to feed your growing families?' He has not just made a negative statement but has instead evoked an emotional response in his audience. They have found themselves agreeing with every statement he has made and are ready to say yes to his next question, whatever it is. If he makes it 'How many of you will join me striking for better wages?" He is almost guaranteed for the whole audience to say 'Yes' as they have to every other one of his questions. You have shown how he feels and you have shown him engaging the other characters. In doing so, you will have drawn the reader in as well.

The same is true when we look at description and scene setting. In a romance your hero might be taking your heroine for a picnic.

'He put the hamper on the hillside and they ate.'

Short, to the point, telling.

'The meadow smelled sweet, as the butterflies flitted between the poppies, dancing in the pools of sunlight as they went. He laid the blanket across the dewey grass and took her hand to lower her down. Her hand felt warm and soft in his gnarled fingers and he held it as gently as though it were a newborn chick. Once he'd unbuckled the leather bindings and the wicker hinges had creaked open, he drew out two crystal flutes and a bottle covered in condensation, testifying to the mouth-watering chill of the champagne.'

This version may be a little over the top in places, but you have the same scene shown. In doing so you've called on the senses, the smell of the meadow, the sound of the hinges, the feel of her hand and so on.

Although of course it is possible to get carried away, showing will evoke far more in the way of response in both your characters and your reader and should be used whenever possible.

> Never show **and** tell the same point

PC: Although both showing and telling have their uses, there is never a case for telling and showing the same point.

'Jane shivered uncontrollably and her skin was blue. "Could I borrow your spare sweater?" she said because she was cold.'

The reader is left thinking you either don't trust your ability to show how Jane feels, or assume they're not intelligent enough to work it out for themselves.

EXERCISE 1

Find an article in a newspaper and rewrite it showing, rather than telling, as much of the information as possible. (You could fictionalise it at the same time and turn it into a story.) Then find an emotional short story, one of yours if you like, and rewrite it reporting only the bare 'facts'.

Can you see how one style is better suited to a factual report where accurate details have to be expressed succinctly and how the other helps create an engaging work of fiction?

EXERCISE 2

Describe two very different people out for a walk together. Perhaps they're different sexes or ages, have different backgrounds or fitness levels. Show their differences without directly referring to them. Their names, the way they speak, what they notice, and frequency with which they stop for breaks can all help with this.

TENSES

RJK: There are many different tenses in language and I do not propose to go through them all in detail. There are plenty of books on the subject if you have the time and inclination to read and learn from them all. However, there are basic rules which every writer needs to be aware of.

Essentially, you can decide to write a story in either the past or the present tense. Although we learn to speak in the present tense before we learn the past, it is much easier to write convincingly in the past tense. The mistake that is often made when writing a story in the present tense is the confusion of introducing past events and whether the story is linear. To remain in the present throughout the story, you cannot dot about between time periods. If you do then you are best to drop into the pluperfect (he had done x, she had said y) and then come back to the present after the historic episode is over.

> 'Joe is enjoying the warm sun on his face. It makes him think of the time in Corfu twenty years ago.
>
> He had gone with his family to a small village away from the main town. They had swum in the sea to cool down in the heat of the day. It had been pure joy to all of them.
>
> He smiles as he picks up his beer and watches his own child playing in the pool.'

Here your story about Joe is in the present, but in a brief flashback you show him remembering what happened in the past. You could have used the past tense instead of the pluperfect, but that is generally used for recent past rather than distant past. It can be confusing to the reader if it reads as though it has only just happened. Here it would read as though you had forgotten you were writing in the present tense and had slipped accidentally.

When writing in the present tense, other than those sections of backstory, if you do not keep the time period linear, you will tie yourself in knots and confuse the reader. For example, if 'now' the present that you are writing is Tuesday 20th May, you cannot, as you progress through the story, talk about something that you did on Monday 19th and still be in the present tense. It is clear that you have gone backwards in time and therefore it cannot, logically, be the present.

When writing in the immediate past tense, then whether you are talking about Monday or Tuesday or alternating between the two you can stay in the same tense, leaving it clear to the reader and without falling into bad habits (or sounding like a footballer being interviewed after the match).

Tenses are also important when writing for children. Young children learn different tenses at different stages of development. It is not appropriate when writing for the under fives to write conditional tenses 'I would be x...' or 'I would have been y...' as these are not learnt until the child is primary school age. It is important to consider what age the child will be when they learn the tenses you use within the story.

Then there is the problem of mixing tenses or using the wrong tense of a verb. There are instances here where American and English differ in what is acceptable. An American one that particularly stands out is the past tense of 'to fit'. In English it is 'fitted', e.g. 'The shirt fitted him well.' American has allowed as acceptable usage 'fit' e.g. 'The shirt fit him well.' I am starting to see writing from English authors where this is creeping in, but to me it remains incorrect.

There are some words where it is not uncommon for people to make mistakes with

> **Be careful where word endings change with tense**

the spellings of tenses. Some are simple errors of spelling others are misunderstandings as to meaning. Take 'He was stood...' as opposed to 'He was standing...' These are not interchangeable. If someone 'was stood' then the action is being done to the subject. In this instance, a third party is standing them somewhere. In 'was standing' it is a description of what the subject is doing. It is a simple action by the subject. Sat and sitting are also frequently mixed up.

There are words which change their spelling in different tenses and some of them trip up many writers. In the above story about Joe and his holiday, when I used the pluperfect I said 'he had swum'. If I had been in the simple past tense then it would have been 'he swam', again, the two are not interchangeable.

Keep tenses consistent

What is most important is to choose the tense you are writing in and then stick to it in those areas which need to be consistent. Of course you will use different tenses, such as the pluperfect in backstory or conditional tenses in things that may or may not happen, but if the main body of your story is in the simple past tense then don't part way through a paragraph or sentence suddenly switch to present. For example:

> 'Joe yawned. Forcing himself to stay awake at 3am is not something he was used to. He swigged his coffee and looks around the darkened room.'

Here Joe's yawning is written in the past tense. Then in the next sentence by using 'is' instead of 'was' we have switched to present and then at the end of the sentence we've switched back to past. We've done the reverse in the next sentence, starting with 'swigged' (past) and coming back to 'looks' which is present. It is easily done and is something you should always check your work for. If you find it hard to spot, then make sure you employ the services of someone who will be able to highlight it for you.

PC: Use of dialogue often trips authors up and they'll continue in the wrong tense after a lengthy discussion.

RJK: I've seen stories where I can guess the precise point the writer set the story aside to come back to later. The first part may be written in past tense and then suddenly part way through there is a shift to everything from there on being in present tense. Rectifying that can be a big job and you cannot expect the place to which you have submitted your work to do that for you. If you get a piece come back from an editor which says something like, 'Please correct the tenses and resubmit' then make sure you go through the whole piece carefully and if you cannot see anything wrong ask someone else to look at it for you, to point out what is meant.

Ensure that your work is consistent and you have structured your sentences correctly to impart what you really mean to say. If you use the wrong tense or the wrong verb ending you will at best change the meaning of what appears on the page and at worst find readers wanting to correct your work.

EXERCISE

As you did with POV, select a scene from a favourite book and rewrite it in a different tense. Are some parts harder to change than others? Think about why that is.

GRAMMAR – WHAT'S THE POINT?

Bear with me as you read this chapter. I'm going to try to show rather than tell why grammar and punctuation are so important.

> intheearlywritingscribeswereusedtotakedownwritingandre
> aditoutagainasrequiredaswithoutanyformofpunctuationthe
> writingwasveryhardforanordinarypersontoworkoutwhere
> onewordstoppedandwherethenextbegan

Some of you may have managed to decipher the above, but for those who didn't, it reads:

In the early writing, scribes were used to taking down writing and read it out again as required. They had to read it back as without any form of punctuation the writing was very hard for an ordinary person to decipher. It was hard to work out where one word stopped and where the next began.

> as writing became something that the ordinary person wished to read spaces were introduced between words but no further punctuation as i have done here

As time moved on, punctuation was used specifically to make the work more readable and the meaning clear to the reader. It is easy to see it as an unnecessary encumbrance, but it is there to assist the reader in understanding the meaning. Let's look at some examples:

Grammar assists the reader understand the meaning

> The most famous example is possibly – Let's eat Grandma – without punctuation we have an instruction to eat Grandma, not something Grandma would be overly

enamoured with.

"Let's eat, Grandma." Now correctly punctuated it is clearly an invitation for Grandma to eat with us.

The order of words is also important in imparting meaning. It is one of the things I am currently struggling with in learning German. In English (and quite possibly in other languages) the sentence structure, if misused, has the potential to change the meaning.

I walked with John wearing a carnation.

Wearing a carnation, I walked with John.

In this example for the first line it is possible to assume that it is John who is wearing the carnation. In the second it is very clear that it is the narrator who is wearing the carnation. It is a subtle but important difference.

Another example of using punctuation to give meaning is the old line:

it was and i said not but

Without punctuation that appears nonsensical. However, add a little punctuation and it becomes:

It was 'and' I said, not 'but'.

Much is written about the impact of texting and its influence on how we write English, but both punctuation and grammar are there to help not hinder the process. There are whole books on how to punctuate correctly and how to use proper grammar; here I can only cover a small amount. The important lesson for the writer is that these are not hurdles put there to make your life more difficult and it is not clever to totally disregard them. They are there to make your writing accessible to everyone, even those who cannot guess what was in your mind when you wrote your masterpiece – they are there to make reading both enjoyable and easy for the reader.

By contrast it is also important not to become hidebound by grammar rules. If your writing becomes more about getting every rule right and not about the flow of the story, then the reader will not go away satisfied. There is a balance to be found. Where that balance sits will depend on the market you are writing for. Some areas have a more informal style than others, where the traditional rules of grammar are adhered to with less enthusiasm. It is also key to be aware that language is a living thing and is not static, neither are the rules which govern it. Once it was unacceptable to write alright instead of all right, now it is fairly widespread and only upsets the more traditional amongst us.

Another which is shifting is the use of conjunctions. Conjunctions are words like 'and', 'but' and 'so' and conjunction means they come at the point of two things coming together. Historically none of these are words which would have started a sentence. They denoted the continuation from a sentence that had already begun. Over time as writing has become more informal this is one of the rules which is being eroded. Even if you are a relative traditionalist there are exceptions to this, where you are showing speech it is not uncommon for people to use them as a way of 'holding the floor' in conversation or of continuing from where another speaker has left of.

I know of one person who, if confronted by a sentence beginning with 'so' would read no further. I accept that is an extreme reaction, but it does show how strongly some feel about the issue. With that in mind, if you do feel the need to start your sentences with any of them, then do so sparingly and don't use them as padding. For example:

> 'So, Joe was walking along the street. But his brother was playing video games.'

If it warrants a new sentence the 'but' could be omitted, and of course the initial 'so' was not needed in the first place.

I find it is even more common for writers of children's literature to use conjunctions at the start as a way to keep sentences short. However, where it is used all the time, this is teaching children bad habits from a young age. For the most part, where a conjunction starts a sentence it can simply be omitted.

Another common one is split infinitives. The infinitive is the basic form of the verb and usually preceded by 'to'; to walk, to read, to cook etc. The rule used to be that splitting infinitives (putting a word between 'to' and the verb) is always wrong, but even before *Star Trek* introduced 'to boldly go' writers have been putting adverbs in the middle of the verb's infinitive. There are times it looks clumsy to do otherwise, but again it's important if you make this choice to understand you have done it deliberately and not simply misplaced the adverb.

Whilst we are on adverbs (in simple terms they are words that modify verbs. For example; run slowly, speak loudly etc.) it is a good time to talk about how many adverbs and adjectives (words that describe nouns – for example; golden hair, wet hands etc.) should be used in your writing. Some people will tell you to remove pretty much all of them. Instead of an adverb, find a stronger verb. Adjectives can very often be removed without any detriment to the writing. For some new writers this sounds absurd. How many of us were asked by English teachers at junior school to see how many descriptive words we could include in our writing? To throw out the ways we were taught can seem extreme. However, the quality of your writing will be improved by ensuring you use them sparingly and only when they serve a useful purpose. If you have a whole string of adjectives the chances are you need to do some serious editing.

> **Instead of an adverb, find a stronger verb**

PC: It might help to remember that we were taught English to make us more aware of the language and help us to pass our exams. Just as shop staff are not expected to show their working when calculating how much change to give, creative writers no longer have to use every device we were taught as teenagers.

RJK: Another rule, which is changing with time, is the use of the subjunctive. This is where you are describing something which is not a known fact. For example, you might say 'If it rains on Thursday...' you don't know it is going to rain. In this case if the sentence is expressed as 'If it was to rain on Thursday...' then the correct use of the subjunctive would make it 'If it were to rain on Thursday...' Which probably makes you glad that it is less rigorously adhered to!

Yet again the writer is faced with a choice. Some writers choose to write oblivious to the rules of grammar, relying on what has become learned behaviour rather than on knowing what the rules behind those behaviours are. That can work, if you were taught well. Otherwise you will bring to your writing all the errors of your own upbringing, schooling and to an extent regional bias.

> If you know the rules you can break them for impact

If you know the rules you can break them for impact. However, if you don't have a good grasp of grammar then you risk errors being picked up by your readers or communicating a meaning other than the one you intended. Grammar is essential as a way to ensure that what you have in mind is exactly what the reader understands. Following rules purely for the sake of them being rules will make your writing stilted, but totally ignoring them will leave it incomprehensible. If it is not your strength, then use a good editor or a friend who has a better understanding to help you.

Punctuation

Punctuation, like grammar, could take up this whole book. There are basic rules that all writers should understand, but there are also much more complex areas that it would help to know. Here we will only cover a couple of things that cause common confusion or are regularly used incorrectly.

Apostrophe

The apostrophe is a sadly abused fellow. Try as he might to help communicate information, he regularly finds himself in the wrong place at the wrong time. I am as

> The apostrophe is a sadly abused fellow

guilty of his abuse as the next person. In one of the books co-authored with my dog, I bowed to his preference for aesthetic purposes, not to include an apostrophe in the name of his Pet Dogs Democratic Party. I've told him it should be Dogs' but he refuses to listen.

If you are contracting a word or words then the apostrophe is inserted to indicate that letters have been removed. Had not becomes hadn't, She will becomes she'll and so on.

The apostrophe is also critical in denoting possession without having to express it the long-winded way. You can say 'The pen belonging to Maggie' or simply 'Maggie's pen'. This is where writers really start to get confused. Although talking about a person like Maggie is easy, what about when it is something belonging to more than one subject? If it were some bowls belonging to the dog I might say 'the dog's bowls' but if I am talking about multiple bowls belonging to multiple dogs it becomes 'the dogs' bowls'. Moving the apostrophe to after the s has shown we are now talking about multiple dogs.

Let's make it even more confusing and use a word that is already plural, such as children. Here, as the word is in itself plural, the apostrophe goes once again before the 's' which here denotes possession. Therefore, it would be 'children's toys'.

Finally, let's look at the one that is most commonly confused. When you are using 'it' as your third person rather than he or she, the rule changes. An item belonging to 'it' does not carry an apostrophe. Here it would be 'its blue eyes' for example. If you see 'it's' it means that it is a contraction of 'it is' and not the possessive form. That one is very easy to get wrong, particularly if you are writing or typing quickly.

PC: It seems wrong to leave out the apostrophe, but if you think of writing his or her blue eyes, you'll see that you wouldn't have her's or his's and so 'its' is correct.

Exclamation mark

Use exclamation marks sparingly

RJK: Exclamation marks are becoming the most over used punctuation mark available. In modern informal writing, texts, emails, adverts, social media posts etc, they are used for emphasis after many sentences and sometimes in a whole line. Unless in your own story you are illustrating what a character is doing in one of those forms of communication, it is very unwise to use exclamation marks, other than infrequently and never more than one at once.

If you crack a joke, then that should be clear without adding an exclamation mark to the end. If you make a point of emphasis, ensure your character's speech pattern or behaviour illustrates that and don't add an exclamation mark. For reference, it is no more acceptable to use them in children's literature than it is in work for adults.

Question mark

I've already said that you don't need multiple exclamation marks, but neither do you need them in conjunction with a question mark. It really is one or the other. If you have included a question then follow it with a question mark and nothing more.

The most common confusion on the question mark appears to be where your character is wondering. 'Joe wondered if he should finish his sentence with a question mark.' This is not a question and is followed by a full stop. If you write it as 'Joe wondered, should he finish his sentence with a question mark?' Now it is a question. You have put a comma after his wondering and then posed a question.

PC: And then there are interobangs. You'll probably never need to use one, but I love the word so much I can't resist trying to sneak in a mention of them. They're a combined question mark and exclamation mark, used for exclamatory questions.

RJK: Interobangs are a relatively recent arrival from America and do not appear in most British punctuation references.

Ellipsis

An ellipsis is three dots in a line denoting something is missing or that there is a pause. It is most

An ellipsis is three dots – no more – no less

often used by writers to denote the breaking off of speech due to interruption or the character pausing to think. It is unnecessary to use multiple strings of dots, just the three will give the same meaning. Some word processing packages will recognise three dots as an ellipsis and automatically space them and count them as one character.

An ellipsis is not normally followed by other speech marks, with the exception of a question mark and closing quotes.

As to whether there are spaces before or after the ellipsis where it appears in the middle of a sentence, that is a matter of the style guide of the publication.

Punctuating speech

What I am about to say relates to the UK. Some USA writers have tried to convince me they were taught differently, but if they were then it is a regional thing in the USA as most conform to this model.

Punctuation relating to speech goes inside the speech marks. All speech requires some punctuation, even if it's just a comma before the speech tag.

As an example:

> All speech requires some punctuation

Toby turned to Florence. "Do you think it's going to rain today?"

"I've got my umbrella, just in case," she said.

He looked out at the blue sky. "Well, I hope you are just being pessimistic. I don't think I'll take a coat."

Another common mistake is to forget to place a comma before a name when addressing someone in speech. As an example, if you are saying "Your grandmother is crazy Wendy." You need to differentiate between when you might be saying "Your grandmother is 'crazy Wendy'" where you are saying that 'crazy Wendy' is the grandmother and when you are talking to Wendy about her grandmother. "Your grandmother is crazy, Wendy." There is a subtle but very important distinction.

Always, if you are addressing someone is speech put a comma

before their name, unless you put their name at the start of the sentence in which case the comma would go after the name. "Wendy, your grandmother is crazy."

(With apologies to all grandmothers of people called Wendy! You are not crazy as far as I am aware.)

At the same time, try to limit the number of times you use the name in speech. When you are talking to someone you do not continue to use their name every time you say something to them. Unless you are using it as a device to remember their name on a first meeting. After this you will only use the name on a limited number of occasions. Listen to conversations and hear how many times a name is used.

Commas

All of the situations in which a comma should or should not be used would take up another book. Some of their usage is a question of perception and some writers and editors prefer more or less. In general terms they should be used to ensure the reader pauses in the right places and to be certain the correct meaning of a sentence is portrayed.

One that is worth looking at is known as the Oxford comma.

Writers could spend all evening discussing their preferences for using or ignoring the Oxford comma. It appears (if used) before the and of the final item in a list. For example: 'Cherries, bananas, apples, and oranges.' Here the last comma, the Oxford comma, may be omitted. Whether it is used may be about house style or personal preference. However, if your list were '*Wuthering Heights, The Adventures of Sherlock Holmes, Great Expectations* and *Pride and Prejudice*' then excluding the comma makes it sound as though a) Pride is a different book from Prejudice and b) you've written it badly by using the word 'and' twice. In that instance the use of an Oxford comma can significantly improve the situation.

There are also instances where the use of the Oxford comma can remove the risk of misunderstandings. If you are giving a list that was for example 'My aunt and uncle, The Queen and Prince Charles' there is a serious risk that the reader thinks that instead of being a list, the second part is a development of the first and your aunt and uncle are in fact The Queen and Prince Charles, which would be unfortunate for a number of reasons. Here you are better either to reword the sentence completely or use the Oxford comma to make it clearer.

Writers do need to keep to hand a good reference book on punctuation and grammar. Even the humble comma has many special rules and it is easy to be accused of both its under and over use as well as using it incorrectly.

EXERCISE

Persuade a friend to copy out a news report or article, leaving out all punctuation marks and capital letters. Now add in the punctuation where you think it should go. Did you make sense of it? Are there any parts which would mean something different if they were punctuated differently? Compare it to the original to see if you missed anything or saw it differently.

CHARACTERS

When you read a story, a character may come across as either 'two-dimensional' or more fully developed and thereby interesting. The art of the writer is to accomplish the latter in a natural and convincing way. There are two parts to this, firstly how well the writer knows the character and secondly how that information is delivered.

> The art of the writer is to create well-rounded characters

When writing a short story, it is possible to create a convincing character, while only knowing aspects of their life which directly affect the snippet you are telling. If, for example, your story is set around the kitchen table, it may be necessary to know what pets there are in the house. Is there a dog water bowl on the floor, or a cat litter tray? It may be relevant to develop the character by knowing that the fine bone china tea service was passed down from their grandmother and that they only use it because of their domineering mother, when really they would rather use stoneware mugs. The latter is not a large piece of information, but it tells you something about their character and their family as well as the china itself. What you probably don't need to know is what school they went to and whether they like music.

Of course, you need to have thought about what they look like. Aspects of their appearance which show their character are as important as the specifics of their hair colour. If their eyebrows grow in natural chaos it will give a different impression than stressing that your character plucks them until they are almost non-existent, although it will only be in conjunction with other attributes that the reader will really start to build a picture. Whether they are dressed in a calf-length, neat, floral dress with an apron or a tight fitting short skirt with tee shirt barely covering their midriff tells you something about their character as well as their appearance.

If we were to convey this information as a block it would be rather dry for the reader.

'Joan sat at the kitchen table. She had brown hair which was permed into neat rolls, and wore a blue floral dress covered by an apron. She was about 5'4" tall and had three sons and a cat.'

The reader is going to yawn and not get excited about Joan.

However, suppose during your story you show Joan kneading dough and wiping her flour covered hands on her already smeared apron? You can show the cat getting under her feet and her having to get the stool to reach the top cupboard.

In doing that you weave the information into the story, building the picture, without the reader being bored.

PC: I agree about weaving in the descriptions. For physical aspects, if they're needed at all, this should be done as soon as possible. The reader will begin to develop their own picture of the character from the start and contradicting this will distance them from the story.

> Weave description into the story naturally

RJK: In writing a novel you may be covering a much longer period of time and certainly have the space to develop your characters more fully. That means knowing a great deal more about them and recording that information so you don't contradict yourself. You can't have the character's blue eyes of chapter one morphing into brown eyes in chapter twelve.

I use a character questionnaire and have each of my characters fill it in at the start of the writing process. The first half of the questionnaire is sensible questions on everything from shoe size, to childhood pets. It's the factual side. Then I move on to the subjective areas that are about the development of character. What are their likes and dislikes? What makes them angry? What is their philosophy on life? What is their worst fear? That last one is very useful if I want to put them in a situation of stress. You can play on a worst fear to create tension.

In total there are about 120 questions that each character who plays a major role has to answer. It's a bit like making each character fill in the regular 'getting to know yourself' questionnaires which appear in many magazines. If you approach it that way, and you can even pretend to be that character as you fill it in, it's more like a bit of fun than knuckling down to work. I don't necessarily use all the information I gather, but it does help to shape how they react in a situation. Once I know their political views, for example, I have an easy way to get them into an argument if I need to. Even for siblings, their view of their upbringing may be completely different.

You want a story from which the reader comes away having felt they have really got to know

> The reader needs to care about the characters

the characters. They care about them and what happens to them. If you can get to the point where the reader feels bereft when your character leaves their life, then you know you have really succeeded in getting the depth of the character across to the reader. There is nothing better than a book where, by the end, you are barely aware of whether the person is just a character in a book or someone you know in real life. When the boundaries of fact and fiction start to blur, then the author can pride themselves on having developed convincing and three-dimensional characters.

To get you started we've included an outline character questionnaire as the next chapter. You can take it and add your own sections as you think of new areas you need to be aware of. Many of the later questions are deliberately quick fire and not to be thought about for ages. As you get deeper into your character they are there to help you start to understand what they would choose and, almost like method acting, think yourself into their place.

PC: Although I can see the value of character questionnaires I don't use them myself. Instead I try to physically put myself in a situation which would be common for the character and then, later, take them out of their comfort zone. It doesn't need to be dramatic; clothes shopping and then visiting someone in hospital would do it.

In each case, I try to notice the things they'd see, rather than what interests me. I relate what happens to examples in their past rather than my own. You could try spending an hour as your character, cook or order yourself the food they'd choose, have a go at their favourite hobby, maybe even buy their clothes from a charity shop.

RJK: It's worth trying both ways and finding what works for you. I have been known to go and have a drink with my character in their 'favourite' pub as part of my research, which is the same sort of thing.

EXERCISE

Use the character questionnaire that follows to develop a fully rounded character for one of your stories. Then reward yourself with a drink at your character's favourite pub!

CHARACTER QUESTIONNAIRE

This has been pulled together from many suggestions and ideas over the years. You don't have to answer all the questions, but the more you know about your character the more depth you can write into them.

- Full Name:
- Maiden Name:
- Nickname:
- Date of Birth:
- Date of Death:
- Place of Birth:
- Place Now Living:
- Type of House:
- Occupation:
- Place of Work:
- Height:
- Hair Colour:
- Describe the character's relationship with his or her boss and colleagues:
- How does the character feel about his or her job?:
- Eye colour:
- Physical appearance:
- Car:
- Medical Conditions:
- Marital Status – Describe the character's romantic life (married, divorced, involved?) and any relevant background (for example previous marriages, affairs):
- Describe the character's sex life and moral beliefs:
- Spouse:
- Pets:
- Does the character have children? If so, describe his or her relationship with them. If not, describe his or her attitude

toward children:

- Distinguishing features:
- Piercings and tattoos:
- Relationship with other characters:
- Interests:
- What is the character's religious background and current religious beliefs:
- What gets them excited?:
- What makes them angry?:
- Describe the character's philosophy in life:
- Describe the character's political views:
- What are their weak spots?:
- What are their faults?:
- Describe the character's childhood in terms of:
    - relationship with parents.
    - relationship with other members of the family.
    - relationship with other key people in his or her youth.
    - lifestyle while growing up.
    - education.
    - childhood hobbies (activities, interests).
- Describe the character's education during and after secondary school. Include any specialist training or military training:
- Describe the character's current relationship with:
    - parents.
    - other members of the family.
    - other key people from his or her youth.
- Sum up the main aspects of the character's personality, including whether he or she is optimistic, pessimistic an introvert or an extrovert, and so forth:
- What is the character proud of?:
- What is the character ashamed of?:
- How intelligent is the character?:
- What is the character's goal in the story?:
- Why does he or she want to achieve this goal?:
- Who or what is trying to stop this character from reaching the goal? Why?:

- What strengths of this character will help him or her in the effort to reach this goal? What weakness will hold him or her back?:
- How articulate is your character?:
- Does the character have an accent or dialect? (If so, describe it):
- Does the character use slang or professional jargon? (If so, describe it):
- Favourite foods?:
- Ever been to Africa?:
- Ever loved someone so much it made them cry?:
- Been in a car accident?:
- Favourite day of the week?:
- Favourite restaurant?:
- Favourite flower?:
- Favourite sport to watch?:
- Favourite drink?:
- Favourite ice cream flavour?:
- Favourite fast food restaurant?:
- Carpet colour in their bedroom?:
- Who did they get their last email from?:
- What do they do most often when they're bored?:
- Bedtime?:
- Favourite TV show?:
- Last person they went out to dinner with?:
- Have they been out of the country?:
- Do they believe in magic?:
- Do they believe in ghosts?:
- What are they listening to right now?:
- Have they ever failed a test, if so what?:
- Do they have a crush on someone?:
- How long have they been with their current partner?:
- What are they wearing right now?:
- Do they smoke?:
- Do they drink?:
- Favourite colours?:
- Favourite animal?:
- Birthmarks?:

- Have they ever been slapped? If so why?:
- Shy or outgoing?:
- Shower or bath?:
- Loved or hated school?:
- Do they have a social life?:
- How easily do they trust people?:
- Do they have a secret people would be surprised to know?:
- Do they like to dance?:
- Do they like to travel?:
- Ever been expelled or suspended from school?:
- Homebird or wanderlust?:
- Ever been dumped?:
- Who do they look up to?:
- Are they a role model?:
- Do you have siblings?:
- How do they vent their anger?:
- Ever run away?:
- Ever been fired from a job?:
- Do they even have a job?:
- Do they daydream?:
- What does their ex look like?:
- Are they rude?:
- Last compliment they received?:
- Lucky number?:
- What does their hair look like right now?:
- Would they date someone younger?:
- Would they date someone older?:
- When was the last time they were drunk?:
- Do they look more like their mother or father?:
- What do they like most about their body?:
- What do they like least about their body?:
- Prefer blondes or brunettes?:
- What size shoe do they wear?:
- Last time they went to a party?:
- Ever been the subject of a rumour?:
- One of their bad qualities?:
- One of their good qualities?:
- Ever been arrested and if so what for?:

- What kind of music do they like?:
- Worst fear?:
- If they had one last word to say to someone before they died, what would it be?:
- Favourite scent?:
- Favourite band?:
- How many languages can they speak?:

PC: If I was doing this I'd be tempted to have the character fill it in, rather than me the author answering for them. The answers might then be even more revealing. E.g. the response to tattoos wouldn't be either 'No' or 'Eagle on left arm', but 'Of course not!' or 'absolutely, there's the regimental crest just here and I'm going to get the kids' names done underneath.'

SPEECH TAGS

Avoid the overuse of speech tags

RJK: Whilst it is important in dialogue for the reader to know who is speaking, it is all too easy to overdo the use of speech tags. Particularly when you only have two characters in a scene, repeatedly writing 'she said' or 'he said' at the end of each line is unlikely to be necessary and will jar with the reader if overused. It is something that many writers do, while others make it worse by using a whole variety of speech tags in place of 'he said', such as 'he whispered', 'he enunciated', 'he screamed' etc. Fancy speech tags, in general, interrupt the flow of the reading. One thing we learn to do in reading is to read past the speech tags when it is a basic 'he said'. Although we recognise it is there and therefore understand who is speaking, unless they are dotted too often through the work, we learn to ignore their existence and the writing continues to flow. If we start hitting terms like 'he expostulated', 'she whispered', it is much more intrusive to the reading.

PC: I've seen, '"Shh," she whispered quietly.' I didn't read on.

RJK: Whilst we are on the subject, it is also a good point to explain that we do not 'laugh' words nor do we 'breathe' them. We might try to say them while laughing, or say them breathily. If you are going to follow speech with 'he laughed' remember it is a new sentence and not the way the words have been said.

It is possible to avoid speech tags altogether, or at the very least keep their usage to a minimum. If it's obvious who is talking, either because you have a limited number of people present and it is clear what the other(s) are doing, or because you have used the actions of the character to define who is in control of the story, then the speech tag is superfluous

Use actions instead of tags

126

and should be removed. What is completely unnecessary is to have "I'm late," Jake said as he put down his pen. If you are going to include the action of Jake putting down his pen then you can use that to tell the reader who was speaking. "I'm late." Jake put down his pen. Until you change paragraph you are indicating to the reader they are with the same character who spoke and therefore they know it is Jake. It is why you need to change paragraph when you change character as the way the work is laid out gives information to the reader which adds to the actual words. If, instead of the above, we had:

"I'm late."
Jake put down his pen

The reader will assume that the character speaking and the one who put down his pen are two different people. Again, a subtle distinction.

These couple of paragraphs have been taken from *The Appearance of Truth*:

"No, thanks, I'm fine with this." She glanced down at the still full glass of wine. "I probably shouldn't be drinking. I didn't have much breakfast."
"Here, have a look at this." Pete passed the Sunday lunch menu to her when he returned with his pint.

In both instances you know exactly who is talking, but there is no speech tag other than the action of the characters. It is also a useful way to weave in your description without giving solid blocks of narrative.

Here is another section from the following page – the conversation goes back and forth between the two, but only once have I resorted to a speech tag of 'she said' or anything similar:

"You nearly didn't." She looked up from the menu. "I don't go in for meeting strange men. Are you eating?"
"I prefer not to think of myself as strange. I'll have the roast beef if you're having something."
"I didn't mean..." she looked back at the menu again,

feeling the colour rise in her face. "I'll have the lasagne," she said without looking up.

She opened her bag and took out her purse. Pete put his hand onto hers. "Please, let me. I know today will be tough. Let this be my treat."

For a moment she stared at him. Her instinct was to argue for equality, but there was something in the gentle firmness of Pete's words that allowed her to accept. "Thank you, that's very kind."

I am not saying speech tags should be completely redundant, far from it, but they do not need to be intrusive and certainly do not need to appear at the end of every phrase of speech. I say 'end' because that is the more normal place for them in modern adult fiction, or partway through the line of dialogue if there is a natural break. In children's books it may be necessary to move them ahead of what is being said to make the reading easier, but as long as your writing is well set out in appropriate paragraphs and your characters are sufficiently deep to be different from each other, then the reader is likely to understand.

EXERCISE

Take one of your stories and rewrite some or all of it replacing basic speech tags with action by the characters. How close can you get to the point where the characters are clearly indicated, your story reads naturally but without any simple tags?

CLICHÉS

PC: A cliché is a saying or phrase which has been overused and shows lack of originality.

> Overusing clichés shows lack of originality

Often they've lost any meaning they originally had and we're so familiar with them we don't even notice their use. It's fine for some of our characters to speak in clichés. That's what people do. However, as authors we really shouldn't write anything without thinking about the impact of our words. Including clichés can show we haven't given enough consideration to what we're writing.

Consider, 'I'd avoid her like the plague', 'She's no better than she should be ', 'He was absolutely over the moon at the news' and 'You could hear a pin drop'. Are they any stronger or more accurate than, 'She has a poor reputation', 'He was delighted' and 'It was quiet'? Better still, show those things to the reader or find a more original way to say it. Perhaps it was so quiet you could hear next door's cat purring, or show him punching the air and offering to buy everyone a pint?

RJK: If you are going to restate a cliché in a more original way, do be careful that in doing so it is neither stilted nor forced. 'Her reputation was not better than a prostitute in a brothel in [insert name of seaport]', might sum your character up, but unless you are writing comedy is too long-winded for the snappy effect that the replacement would need to have. Similarly, don't restate a cliché by trying to cleverly say the same thing, but without the actual words 'He was over the stars' does not make an effective and acceptable replacement for 'He was over the moon'.

Other meaningless phrases

PC: Again, we use these in speech without realising we're doing it. Our characters can do that, but we shouldn't. 'The fact of the matter is', that 'at the end of the day', 'when all's said and done', we don't need them. 'At some point in time', you're going to have to 'take a long hard look at yourself' decide 'enough is enough' and cut these from your work.

Plot clichés and overworked storylines

> Avoid overused phrases... and plots

Have you heard that joke about little Timmy who doesn't want to go to school and his mum says he must because he's the teacher? Well, so has everyone else. If listening to the same joke several times is annoying, just think how an editor feels when she gets yet another version of a story she's familiar with. This happens so often that many publications give lists of storylines to avoid. Read up on these and be sure not to use them.

Reworking an idea which others are likely to be familiar with isn't necessarily plagiarism or a breach of copyright, but it probably won't result in a fresh and engaging piece of writing. That almost certainly means it won't sell or win a prize.

Some general outlines do recur. In a crime story the detective may initially suspect the wrong person and in a romance something will keep the potential lovers apart, otherwise the story will be very short. Even when using these accepted devices, do try to be original and plausible. Don't give your heroine some 'secret' she keeps from the hero, when there's no real reason for her not to tell him and which, when revealed at the end, is something he's not bothered about anyway. If she's so desperately in love, why wouldn't she say she might not be able to have children, explain her family background or admit to a past failing?

RJK: Don't be completely put off however. There are only a limited number of plot lines you can follow. Revenge, betrayal etc. You are not going to think of a completely original plot. However, within that, how you tell it and the directions your characters take can cover a limitless number of paths. One thing you need to do if you are working to a theme is come up with a number of ideas and then rule out the ones that most obviously come to mind unless you have a truly original spin on the subject.

New clichés

PC: Mobile phones are annoying for authors. When your main character gets stuck, they could use theirs to get help. That doesn't help us, so we make sure they forget to charge it up. As that is now becoming a cliché we're going to have to think of something else.

Sat-navs and Google are quite irritating too. If your character would use them, then you'll have to use your imagination to create problems which a quick 'select alternative route' or internet search can't solve. Don't rely on the soon to be considered clichéd lack of signal.

RJK: The sat-nav in my current car once tried to take me from York to Birmingham via Manchester which would have made a minimum two hour journey into at least three hours. It can happen, but using it in a story would depend on my character having no idea of geography and having an out of date sat-nav, which, would then need to be consistent with the rest of the story.

Don't expect to rule clichés out altogether. Use them only where they are genuinely the best way to demonstrate an image to your reader and in a way which does not jar as unoriginal.

EXERCISE

Think of your five most used clichéd phrases (we all have them) and come up with alternatives which, without being contrived, say the same things in a more interesting way.

KEEPING GOING

PC: Once we've got started as writers, there are a number of things which can hinder our progress. Shortage of ideas and the resources to get going have been covered already and later there's a section to help with a lack of time to devote to your writing. Once these things have been overcome, it's often the authors themselves who are the culprits.

Writer's block

Writer's block is a mysterious complaint, the main symptom of which is to be unable to write when there seems no reason not to put words on the page. It's horrible and the fear of many authors. I'm not at all sure it exists.

I don't mean I can always open my laptop and have the words flow effortlessly, or those who say they're blocked are wrong, just that there isn't a particular struggle to get on with things which is exclusive to writers.

> Don't use 'writer's block' as an excuse

Whatever you do, there are times when you're less inclined to do it. Usually we have to carry on regardless. You can't have parent's block and not feed the children, or not bother going to work. Sometimes your efforts will be less well rewarded, the cake won't rise properly, you'll fail to complete your run as fast as usual. Ever heard of baker or jogger's block?

What's often referred to as writer's block is a combination of lack of motivation and procrastination.

RJK: There is a danger in dubbing it 'writer's block' in that you then use it as a neat get-out clause. 'Oh, I don't need to do any today, I've got writer's block'. If you don't feel emotionally, mentally or physically strong enough to continue writing what you were working on, then write something else until you do! Review every book you've ever read, write a letter of complaint, simply write how you're feeling and why – but keep writing!

Lost motivation. How it happens

PC: When we start writing we're often highly motivated. We have ideas we're enthusiastic to write about, perhaps have visions of earning money or praise. Then problems arise. Maybe we discover plot holes, realise we don't really know where our story is going or start to doubt the idea is sufficiently interesting. Or we're happy with what we've written so far, but see it's going to take months or years to complete.

Perhaps we do finish something and we're either dissatisfied with it ourselves, or it meets with criticism, or rejection by publisher after publisher. It doesn't seem worth working on, or starting anything new if that will face the same fate.

Keeping it under control

It helps to be as realistic as possible from the start. Writing takes a long time, both to learn the craft and then to finish each piece. There's no guarantee of financial success. By all means hope to earn money from your stories, but if that's your only reason for writing you'd be much better off asking for extra shifts at work or searching the beach with a metal detector.

> Writing takes time

Don't expect constant praise and encouragement from non-writing family and friends. I expect you want them to do well and enjoy whatever interests them. Do you follow every round of golf giving tips for improvement, attend all their piano lessons and afterwards wax lyrical on the beauty of their music, or go shopping with them and enthusiastically admire every single pair of shoes on the High Street? If not, it's unfair to expect them to read all your work, telling you they love it and where you missed a comma.

Equally, don't be put off by people asking if you're still

wasting your time on writing, or saying they haven't seen anything of yours in Waterstones' yet. Put those people into a story… as the victim. RJK: but change their names!

PC: It's only natural we want our work to be published. That's achievable if; we're realistic about who we send it to, get it as near to perfect as possible beforehand, and are incredibly persistent. Rough drafts and poorly targeted submissions will be rejected. Sadly, so will many polished and well-aimed pieces! Keep writing, improving and submitting: that's the most effective route to success.

> Rough drafts and poorly targeted submissions will be rejected

Procrastination

The dictionary says procrastination is the practice of carrying out less urgent tasks in preference to more urgent ones, or doing things we like rather than things we don't. It's putting off tasks until we're forced into them. Sound familiar?

I'm sure we've all procrastinated at some point. It's perfectly understandable that we avoid housework when we could instead read a book in the garden. But what about writing? We want to write, don't we? For many people writing time is precious – yet we spend half of it tidying the desk or cleaning the bathroom. Why?

Partly it's habit. We get used to doing something else before the main event. Stretches before exercising, coffee and a gossip before starting work for the day. Habits can be broken.

Partly it's fear. We can be daunted by the task of finishing a long piece, worried we're not doing justice to our good idea, concerned we'll never get it published. These concerns are perfectly understandable, but shouldn't be allowed to rob us of our chance at success. We can't finish and then sell a piece we never start, can we?

How do we overcome these issues?

Often we just need a little push to get us started. Some people find it helps to finish each section in the middle of a scene, even halfway through a sentence. Others use the 'morning pages' approach. For this simply write for ten minutes on waking up, possibly even before getting out of bed. Just write anything

Do it.
And do it now!

which comes to mind, whether connected with a current work in progress (WIP) or not. The idea is to clear our minds of anything which could hinder our writing.

Another idea is to have a pre-writing ritual. It could be making tea in a particular mug or putting on our lucky socks, anything which doesn't take long and gets us in the mood to write. A plot worked out in advance, even a very rough one can stop us feeling totally lost. Having several projects on the go can also help. If we feel stuck with one, we might be able to work on another. If it's a particular scene causing trouble, then skip it and come back to it later.

Once we've built up a selection of work, it's good for our morale to have several pieces under consideration or entered into competitions. That way there's a chance the next email or post could bring good news.

Keep a record of any long listings, kindly worded rejections from editors or other near misses and of course any successes. Focus on these responses rather than any which are less favourable.

How about trying something completely different? A letter to the local paper or short filler piece for a magazine, such as a household tip or amusing anecdote. These don't take long and getting one into print could be a huge boost to your confidence.

RJK: When I left my former career to write full-time, I wanted to find a way to make sure I did some productive work every single day. I started Alfie's Diary, my dog's internet blog, with the intention of keeping it going for that first year or two. I've missed one day in the last ten and a half years and that was due to unexpected hospitalisation. It's only 300 words a day, but it's won awards and has followers all over the world. You just never know where a writing exercise is going to lead!

Be professional

PC: Just as non-writers aren't allowed to get 'blocked' doing the day job, writers can think of writing as a self-employed occupation (part or full-time). Set working hours and be accountable to yourself. If you've said you'll write at seven this evening, then start tapping your watch at two minutes

> Set working hours and make yourself accountable

to, glare pointedly at your desk with a minute to go and jolly well have the document open and fingers on the keyboard at seven on the dot. And keep them there, and moving, until the story is written or your time is up. If you don't, you'll have to give yourself a very serious talking to and that won't be any fun at all.

Hidden procrastination

There are things we convince ourselves are helping our writing, when really they're doing quite the opposite. Such as reading about Henry VIII's childhood when we only needed to know in which month he was born, or deciding what we'll eat at lunch with our agent before we've finished the first draft.

When I wanted the dictionary definition of procrastination, I could have typed the word into Google instead of fetching the dictionary and looking it up. That sounds quicker, but when I activated the wifi my emails would have downloaded and I'd have checked to see if there was anything important and read all the unimportant ones too. Emails, even exciting ones from editors, can almost always wait an hour or two while you write.

Another problem is pseudo work. We're told writers should be well read, they should have an internet presence and they should network with other writers. That's all true. Critically reading in the genre you write, creating a simple website and exchanging critiques with writing friends all help with our writing. Reading gossip magazines, playing Candy Crush or drinking margaritas with fellow writers don't. I'm not saying we should never do these things, but we should get the writing done first.

If you're serious about writing, prove it to yourself, and others, by making it a priority. Next time you're about to do something other than write, stop and think if it's more important to you than writing. If it isn't, finish the story first.

EXERCISE

Spend the next half an hour writing – no excuses!

ENDINGS

RJK: Every story needs an ending.

That might sound obvious but an end isn't just the last word of the story that you type, or the words 'The End' typed on the page. An ending must be satisfying and appropriate to the story you are writing. It must complete the 'story arc', and I'll explain what that is in a moment. It must also be appropriate to the genre you are writing in.

If you are writing a story to make people feel good, then whilst the death of your lead character might be a natural possible outcome of what has gone before, it is more likely that their recovery to full health is going to be a better fit. If you have been writing a ghost story based on the possibility it might all be real, or it might be perfectly explained by other things, the reader will not be satisfied by you ending saying, 'It was Joe playing a practical joke and ghosts aren't real anyway.' The whole premise of the story is that they might be and you still need to leave the reader with that thought.

> Your ending must fall naturally out of the events which have gone before

Your ending must fall naturally out of the events which have gone before. This is where many writers of stories with a twist make a mistake. It is not all right to suddenly introduce new information, that you have not alluded to in any way previously, just to create a twist ending. The reader will go away feeling cheated and dissatisfied, rather than feeling reading the story was time well spent. This is also why the whole 'it was all a dream' ending rarely works. If you ever had a special balloon that you clutched in your tiny hot hands as a child, which was your pride and joy; then these sorts of ending are much the same feeling as someone coming along and maliciously bursting it.

As part of finishing your book, or story, you need to think about whether the loose ends have been tied up. That does not mean the final page should be a recap of all the characters and situations and a summary of what happened to them, or how things turned out. However, you do need to think about drawing the strands together as you go through your story. Earlier, when talking about openings, I made reference to Lee Child's *Without Fail*, it's also a book worth reading when looking at how the whole story should come together. As you read the book you will find it a perfect example of making everything count. Nothing you are told is without reason. There are no loose ends. By the end of the book everything has been tied up and all the clues have been brought in. Lee Child is remarkably good at writing crime thrillers which give the readers the information so they can be the detective. If you sat down with a pen and paper and looked at it as a detective might, there is every chance you would arrive at the answer with or ahead of his investigator, Jack Reacher. Nothing comes out of left field and nothing is withheld. What is remarkable is, that having said all that, the plots are neither obvious nor easy to unravel. They have enough depth to keep you scratching your head.

Whilst we are not all writing crime fiction, the premise remains the same. The ending is the point where you bring your story together and wrap it up in a way that is satisfying to the reader. It also needs to end with impact and not simply fizzle out. Very often, the reader's desire to immediately pick up your next work will be based on the impact of your ending. In some cases that means finishing on a high, but that is not appropriate in all genres. What is always relevant is to finish in a way that is memorable and gives the reader cause to stay in the moment with the book, before moving on to the next thing in their life.

EXERCISE

In a group, or with a friend, read the final paragraph of a book /story, and some chapter section endings. Can you tell which are intended to encourage you to turn the page and which conclude the story? Try the same thing with some of your own work.

STORY ARC

What then is the 'Story arc'?

The end of your story needs to come round to meet the beginning. If you start with Joe Bloggs facing redundancy, then the story is not going to be complete by finishing with Jane Doe going shopping. The reader wants to know 'what happens to Joe?' and as a writer it is your duty to tell them. You can leave some aspects ambiguous, but you can't go off at a tangent and end in a different place.

> Normally, you will finish with your lead character and the resolution of their problem

In general terms you will finish with your lead character and the resolution of their problem, in the same way that you started with that person and setting out what they needed to deal with. Of course there are exceptions, if you start with an opening body, although you are going to end with the resolution of the crime, it may not be the body itself that you finish with. However, if your story is about who is killing people, and why, then that is the point you need to resolve in your ending.

It is important to know what story you are telling in order to be able to wrap it up satisfactorily. Make sure that early on you have not only thought about plot, and where appropriate sub-plots, but also the point your story is making. I'm not necessarily talking about moral points as some children's stories set out to make, such as 'it's wrong to steal', I'm talking about what the story set out to achieve. What is the theme? If your theme is that friendship can conquer all, then your story is not going to leave the former best-friends hating each other. If your theme is that love can find a way at any age, don't leave your characters still single.

You won't always spell out exactly what happened next. You

may leave your reader with a more open ending, where either they need to fill in the blanks for themselves or wait for your sequel to come out. However, what you do in that situation is leave them enough resolution to show the possibilities. In *The Lifetracer* whilst the initial problem of who is sending death threats has been resolved, I leave the sub-plot of the investigator's relationship with his young son, and the mother standing in the way of them seeing each other, open. Connor walks away heartbroken as Mikey watches him through the window. If I write another novel with Connor then I will pick up the thread of his relationship with Mikey as part of it. It is a continuing story within the overall story framework.

PC: However, each book should still be a complete story in its own right. If we were to read one out of sequence it shouldn't seem to end (or even start) part way through.

RJK: Along the way your characters will have tackled challenges. They will have found a resolution to the problems they faced along the way. The ending is not always a happy one, again it depends on the genre, and your character may not come out winning accolades and bravery awards, but one way or another they will have played a key role in overcoming the challenge and resolving the situation.

EDITING AND PROOFREADING

Editing and proofreading of your work are vital. That is not only true if you are poor at grammar and spelling, but applies whatever stage and capability you are at. We all make mistakes.

There are some things you can do to self-edit your work, but even after that it is best to go through at least one third party, or more if there is an opportunity. There are specialists you can employ to do these functions and their quality and prices vary significantly. It is best, if you are planning to go down that route, to ask for a recommendation. Find someone who knows the genre you are writing in. If you are writing in a specialist field it is best, though not always possible, to find someone who has at least some understanding of that area. If you are planning to publish your own work it is even more vital that it is absolutely correct. Your reviews will depend on it. If you are trying to secure a publisher you do want your work to be the best it can be, but a good publisher will perform some of those functions themselves before publication.

What can you do to edit your own work?

1. The first point may sound obvious, but it is surprising how many people do not do it. Read your work through a second time and correct the errors you find. What stage you do this will vary. Some writers read back over what they have written immediately after finishing writing. Some come back to it the following day. Some wait until the piece is finished and then go through it as a whole. There is no one correct way, do what works for you.

2. Put your work aside for a while and then come back to it again when you are no longer so close to your characters. That's not always easy as characters can tend to stay with you. The point is that you need to come back to your work as a reader, rather

than as the writer. Can you spot the weaknesses in the story? Does it hook you? Is it predictable? Go through with a checklist asking yourself if your work meets all the key points. You can use the chapters of this book as a guide.

PC: I find it helps to write something new before this read through, as that helps give me some distance from the piece.

3. RJK: This is where being part of a critiquing group is immensely helpful. Turn your work over to your critique group for their views. You need to be prepared for whatever criticism comes back and don't be precious about your work. At this stage your colleagues are acting as readers and they are telling you what didn't work for them. If you are going to send your work out for publication it is far better to hear it at this stage when you can still do something about it, than to receive a rejection notice.

> Relocate your darlings rather than murdering them

You need to be prepared to be brutal if necessary. You may have heard the expression 'kill your darlings'. That is not a call to kill your lead character but to be prepared to cut those sentences and paragraphs you so enjoyed writing, but actually don't work for the reader. If you like them that much, rather than deleting them altogether move them to a separate file on your computer called 'darlings'. You can then come back and look at them fondly at a later date and maybe they will inspire another story. It doesn't feel quite so painful if you pension them off, rather than brutally murdering them.

PC: I do this. On one occasion I cut an entire scene from a novel and later used it as the basis of a short story.

4. RJK: After doing all the above you have not finished. The final stage is to read your work aloud. When you read aloud you use a different part of your brain than when you read silently. As a result, whilst it is very easy to read past mistakes when you read silently (your brain corrects things as it reads), you are much more likely to falter on the errors when reading aloud. You will also pick up missing punctuation, as you will trip up reading at those

points. Some people put their work onto a different device to read it too, seeing it differently helps them to spot things. That can be as simple as printing it out and working from a paper copy or transferring it to your kindle. Whatever you do, reading it aloud is an essential part of the process.

PC: Don't be fooled into thinking that because you're sending your work to an editor or proofreader that you don't need to bother with yourself. There's no point paying someone to fix errors you could have corrected yourself – and submitting work which isn't as good as you can make it is an even bigger mistake.

I use Anne Rainbow's RedPen system. It's a step by step approach which breaks the job down into smaller tasks.

EXERCISE 1

Find a story or piece of writing you wrote a while ago and read it aloud to see if you can find errors you missed previously.

EXERCISE 2

Many mistakes and weaknesses are common. When giving feedback on someone else's work, make a note of the things you've suggested they improve and try to take your own advice.

PRESENTING YOUR WORK

RJK: How your submitted work is presented is very important. It's another area where times have changed and if you are still using the rules from the days of typewriters then you may well need to make a few changes. A computer word processing package already builds in many of the things needed to present work well and it is worth getting to grips with whatever package you use to make the most of it. The relative importance of the items which follow will depend on where you are presenting your work to and in what form. If you are sending off paper copies then the overall look is important, but how you achieve it may not be so critical. However, if you are sending your work electronically then you need to be aware of how easy it is for the recipient to use the files you send. The easier you make the life of an editor or publisher the happier they will be to work with you next time.

Don't use a computer like a typewriter

Don't use a computer like a typewriter

1. **Headers and Footers** – Headers should go in the area at the top of the page which is specially designed for that purpose. Do not include them in the body of the page. The same is true of footers at the bottom, including the page number. If you include them in the body of the page then, once the story has been accepted, it is not possible for the story to be copied and pasted into a pre-formatted template without further work. This is the same point I will make with regards to some of the other layout issues below. It means manual intervention to go through and remove the headers and footers which appear in amongst the story text. Whilst this alone is not a lengthy process, once you multiply that by a number of

145

stories and have the risk you might miss one and there might be a random page number appearing in the middle of a story, then you will start to see that the best way to top and tail your story is to use the header and footer function in your word processing package.

PC: Also if you use different software from the recipient, unless you use the header and footer functions, what you include probably won't actually be at the top and bottom of the pages.

RJK: The problem is deeper than that. The same can happen if you are using the same software as they may have their margins set differently, so the text will take up a longer or shorter area.

2. RJK: **Line spacing** – By all means use 1.5 or double line spacing, but never use your return key to do that with an extra line of blank space as you would have done with a typewriter. Doing that will create two problems. Firstly, someone will have to go through and manually delete the extra blank lines. Secondly they will need to ensure that the preceding and following words neither join together or have multiple spaces between them. In some instances, complex 'find and replace' commands can be used, but often it is a manual process and a very time consuming one. In order to introduce the line spacing you want, learn how the function in your word processing package works. The beauty of this is it is easy to adjust if you submit work to multiple places which have different requirements.

3. **Tabs and indents** – Never, never, never, use the space bar to create tabs and indents. If you do that then it is highly likely you will not end up with five spaces (or whatever number, every time) and your work will look ragged. Trust me, I've spent hours using find and replace to get rid of these in documents and even the most careful writer loses count on some occasions. This is another hangover from typewriter days. A word processing package will set those for you where you need them for new paragraphs.

> Don't use the space bar to create indents

PC: Again doing this will make things far quicker and easier for you to comply with differing submission requirements.

RJK: If you have ever set an ebook (more on that later) then you will also be aware that if you include tabs at any point in your document, other than ones correctly set by the word processing package, then it is very likely to throw your formatting out, and if you use Smashwords, it will lead to the whole file failing Autovetter. There will be a function in your word processor to 'show all non-printing characters', if you turn that on you will see marked all the spacing, tabs, line breaks etc., which makes it easier to strip them out. Better still don't include them in the first place.

4. **Paragraph spacing** – Like line spacing and indents, set this within the programme. You do not want an extra blank line before a new paragraph. With a computer there are better ways to get your spacing right. Time taken to really learn the capability of your word processing package will be time well spent.

Make sure when you change from character to character in movement and speech that you start a new paragraph for them. Don't just send the editor a mass of text broken apparently at random. If you don't know how fiction should be laid out then take half a dozen books off the shelf, or buy some magazines and learn from them. Read the appropriate sections of this book too.

Fonts

Make your work easy to read

When presenting your work, how it looks on the page is important. If you are submitting in paper format then use a font that is easy to read on paper. The serif fonts, Times New Roman and Patatino Linotype being good examples, are often easier to read on paper and are generally used within books and newspapers. On screen is a different matter. If you are submitting electronically then use one of the cleaner sans serif fonts, such as Calibri. However, be aware of the submission requirements of the particular publisher the story is going to. If they say 'use Times New Roman' then do that and nothing else.

In terms of the size of the font, generally use 12pt unless otherwise specified.

There are times that you might vary these rules, but only do so for a very good reason. Even if your story includes a letter for which you want to use a handwriting font, then it may be better to include this information as a note rather than trying to produce a fancy layout.

It is not particularly clever to use 'Courier New' to make your work look as though it has been typewritten. At best it will look as though you have not moved on and at worst be very irritating to an editor. As for starting to introduce fancy fonts, this is no more sensible than to handwrite your manuscript on kitchen roll to submit it. Make it look professional and business like. At the end of the day your writing is a business, even if it is a hobby and being professional in your approach will affect how an editor views your work.

PC: If you feel your work needs a fancy font, coloured paper or any other gimmick to make it seem interesting, then what it really needs is to be re-written.

Word count

RJK: Take notice of the word count requirements. If you are told you must write a minimum of 500 words, then that is the minimum length for your story. It is not a figure which should include your name, address, the story title, the name of your cat and your shoe size. If you are given a 'maximum' don't presume that is open to interpretation and send something even one word longer. If a publisher means 'about 1000 words' then that is what they will say and you can allow a small margin, normally not more than 10 % either side. If they give you a word range, then stay within it. They are telling you this for a reason.

> Take notice of word count requirements

However, it is not always quite as straightforward as that. Normally, unless told otherwise, the title is not included in the word count. You might also find that some word processing packages will count your work slightly differently to others. The reason can be as simple as the way it sets out some punctuation and whether it then counts that as words. For example, if you have left a line of space to denote a scene break that won't count as words, however if you put something like ### in the middle of the line then some packages will count a word, put spaces between them and they might count more than one word. If you are told to enter a piece of 'exactly' 100 words then the only safe option is to count them. If there is an upper or lower limit and you are close to it, then carefully review your work to make sure there is nothing which might be miscounted.

Accompanying letter or email

Your email or letter is your opening gambit. If you have made errors of grammar, spelling and punctuation, in that introduction, the reader may not get as far as your story and if they do, they will be starting with the assumption that you can't write! Don't let yourself down.

I've even received work in which the title of the story has been spelled incorrectly in the introductory email. It does not auger well.

The presentation of your work is the first thing an editor is going to see. Before they read a single word they will see your letter or email of submission. This is your chance to show you are professional and serious about your writing. It is not the time to use a flowery bordered paper or email template – you are writing to a professional publisher not to your grandmother. Nor is it the time to choose an outlandish font either in terms of size of appearance. You need to think very carefully about the impression you give.

Presentation of your work is VERY important.

EXERCISE

Take some time to get to know your word processing package properly. If you've never tried setting headers, footers, paragraph spacing etc., then try now to format a document using the built in functions.

FEEDBACK

What is feedback?

PC: A book thrown across the room or reader falling asleep during the opening paragraph could be considered feedback. To really help the writer though, it should be more detailed and specific.

A critique, formal or otherwise, saying what the reader felt did and, perhaps more importantly, didn't work for them is what we need. These must be honest to be of use; empty praise or unjust criticism aren't feedback. The more specific it is the better. "This is boring in places," helps a bit, but, "I really wanted to skip those four pages describing the ice melting in her drink," is even more useful.

> Feedback should be honest and constructive

Reviews are also a form of feedback and very valuable to authors (please do leave a review if you enjoy any of our books!) As these come rather too late to improve that particular piece of work the feedback I'll be referring to here is that received prior to publication.

Why do we need feedback?

Without feedback we're working in a vacuum. We can't judge if our writing is good and if we're improving. Spotting our own mistakes is notoriously difficult. It doesn't matter if they're a misplaced comma, or enormous plot hole, if we wrote them they know how to hide from us. If we can't see them, we can't fix them. It's not easy to know if jokes are funny until we tell them to blank faces or belly laughs. We won't know if characters are likeable until we introduce them to readers.

If we're writing only for ourselves with no intention of ever widening our readership, our reaction is the only feedback we need. If everything we write is snapped up by publishers and lauded with accolades that's feedback enough. Most writers fall somewhere between these two extremes.

Good feedback will highlight our strengths and weaknesses, allowing us to make the most of our writing skills and increase our chances of success. This applies to all writers, no matter how experienced. Any of my stories which I'm at all unsure about are shown to the critique group I belong to and I greatly appreciate their input. Most authors I know do something similar. Even really famous novelists with several bestsellers to their name are likely to have beta readers helping ensure standards don't slip. Agents and editors will also give feedback if there are any areas of an accepted story which require attention.

How do we get good feedback?

Think carefully about who to ask. Everyone is entitled to an opinion, but, when it comes to improving our writing, some opinions are more valuable than others. An avid reader of our genre, even without writing experience or literary qualifications might give useful pointers about how enjoyable the story is and how well it meets expectations. A friend with an English degree, who thinks romances are stupid could help with grammar, but probably won't be a good indication of how well the storyline of our latest bodice ripper works.

Your friends or family may be wonderful providers of honest, helpful feedback and be delighted to give up their time to help you. If that's the case you're very lucky. Do bake them cakes, pick them flowers or take them on two-for-one cocktail nights to show your gratitude.

> Flattery is not the same as feedback

On the other hand, those closest to you may be more inclined to say, "That's lovely dear," to every offering including shopping lists. Or perhaps it'll be, "I don't know why you're wasting your time with that rubbish." If that's the case you're better off not asking them again.

Don't be hard on friends and family members who don't have the time to read your work, or simply don't want to. Will you always be thrilled to hear every detail of their model railway and proofread their timetables when you have a deadline looming?

Other writers are a good source of feedback for a number of reasons. They're likely to have opinions and be able to express them. They'll probably have an idea of the kind of feedback that's needed (and want some in return). With luck they'll also be familiar with the market you're aiming towards.

Where can we find other writers?

Joining a writing group or class is a good way of getting in touch with writers and of obtaining feedback. If you have the opportunity to read your work out, please do just that and only that. If you need to explain first, then it doesn't work. Don't apologise for your story or run it down either. It's irritating and reduces the time available to give feedback.

> Work with other writers to critique each other's stories

Classes and workshops always provide some feedback. Groups may not, or might be too 'nice' to be truly helpful. If that's the case either ask the group leader if more feedback can be given, or ask one or more of the members if they'd like to exchange critiques.

Online groups (or forums) are just as good for this purpose as those where members meet face to face. Actually they're frequently better. Members can read and give feedback at their leisure, so feedback might well be more in depth, rather than an overall impression. The author too can take their time digesting any comments and can go back to refer to them later.

Facebook and LinkedIn host a multitude of different writing groups, an internet search will bring up more, as will requests through Twitter and on blogs. Do check who can read your work. If it's an open site the work could, theoretically, be read by anyone and be considered as published by editors and competition organisers, which limits options for placing those stories. Some sites and forums are hosted by big name publishers. As well as useful feedback these theoretically offer the potential for work to be 'discovered' by the companies involved.

It will probably be necessary to try several groups or sites before you discover which works best for you. Eventually you'll find a writing buddy or buddies, with whom you regularly exchange feedback and support, either in person or via the internet. (You may even end up co-writing a book with one of them – Rosemary and I 'met' via a forum and from there joined the same online group).

Other ways to obtain feedback

Some writing competitions give feedback, either as standard or for a small extra fee. As a prize for being runner-up in a free writing competition I once received feedback from the publishers Curtis Brown, which clearly explained the changes I'd have to make before submitting to them. Opportunities such as this aren't uncommon. My blog, www.patsy-collins.blogspot.com provides regular links to free writing contests.

Since then I've judged competitions myself and have informed entrants why I did or did not place their work in one of the top positions. Often such competitions will command an entry fee. That's likely to be no more than the cost of a paperback and you could end up with valuable insight into your work, or even a cash prize. Competition feedback is especially beneficial if the competition is a regular one, or the feedback provider is likely to judge future competitions which you'll enter.

Submitting your work is likely to result in some kind of feedback. An acceptance, particularly a paid one, is a reliable indication that the work is good. One rejection doesn't mean it isn't, but a regular stream of them for the same piece might suggest something isn't quite right. Some places will give a specific reason for rejection. If that's one of a small range of standard rejection letters, then it may, or may not, help. If it's clearly been written for your story, then take heed; it's useful information.

In some cases, where work shows promise, authors will be given suggestions for improvement and invited to resubmit when these have been made.

> Always see feedback from an editor as a good thing

Never feel that feedback from an editor is a bad thing. It's an extremely good sign as, unless the story has the potential for publication, it's not worth their while to do more than send a standard rejection. Editors simply don't have time to critique every submission.

Another way to get feedback is to pay for it. Prices and services vary widely, so it makes sense to ask around before making your decision. Think carefully about what you want. Proofreaders will spot spelling mistakes, grammatical errors and inconsistencies such as characters mysteriously changing name or going upstairs in a bungalow. An editor, usually for a higher fee, will advise on a range of issues including the structure, style and marketability of your story. They may suggest major changes and the finished work might be a collaboration between them and the author.

Feedback on other people's work can also be useful. Book reviews or comments from judges will often reveal common themes. Publishers and magazine editors often provide lists of mistakes and plot lines to avoid.

How to give feedback

If we want good, regular feedback from writers, we will almost certainly have to pay for it, usually by providing the same service in return. Commenting on another person's work for the first time can be daunting. It's tempting, but not helpful, to

> For good, regular feedback, we will have to provide the same service in return

give only praise. In order to be helpful you really must point out flaws too. You might like to adopt the bad news sandwich strategy of saying something nice, then mentioning something which doesn't quite work and then softening the blow with another positive remark.

Give the kind of feedback you'd like yourself. Be as specific as possible. Say why you disliked a character, exactly where you lost interest, which facts are inaccurate. If you can think of a solution to a problem offer it, but don't be afraid to mention things which won't be easy to fix. Don't ignore typos and small details either. They're the hardest for the author to spot, but the easiest to fix once we're made aware of them.

How to make use of feedback

It's important we're prepared for the level of feedback we've asked for and to use it wisely. If we're not willing to alter our work and make improvements, or are going to take anything but praise as a personal insult then it's not fair to ask for advice. That doesn't mean we must follow all the advice we receive, simply that we should consider it. Only ever make changes you agree with.

RJK: Sometimes it is worth reading the feedback and coming back to make the changes later when you've got over feeling defensive of your work.

PC: At times we immediately see the reader is correct and are happy to make the change. Often the decision isn't so clear cut, especially if big alterations are suggested. We might need to think about it for a while, or try the suggested rewrite whilst keeping the original in case we don't feel the changes work. We might even disagree with suggestions, or see the point but not wish to act on them. That's all O.K.; it's our work and up to us how we write it.

If we obtain advice from more than one source, there are likely to be conflicts. That's good as the writer is forced to make the decision and it reminds us that often there isn't just one correct way to express something.

A word of caution; don't seek out so much feedback that you get confused, or follow so much that you lose your own voice or style. Use it to help you write your own piece your way, not to write like someone else.

If you're fortunate enough to have the piece accepted, you may well want to let your critiquers know they contributed to your success. Finally, always thank the person who gave you feedback, even if it wasn't quite what you wanted to hear. They took time and trouble to try to help you, thanking them is quick and easy.

Giving and receiving feedback

RJK: Because feedback on your work is so important, Patsy and I decided we would both write sections to cover different aspects. We are aware there is some duplication, but have included this so you can really get to grips with what is an essential process in improving your work.

Feedback should be honest, thorough and constructive. When giving feedback it is worth checking with the other members of the group what they are looking for. Some may appreciate having every spelling mistake and punctuation error pointed out, whilst others may be looking only for a higher level comment on what does and does not work within a piece.

Whether you are giving or receiving feedback there are some key points to consider:

1. Little is gained by saying either 'I really like this piece' or 'I don't like this' without giving an explanation.

2. Comment on what has worked within the piece as well as what needs improving. Not only will this help the writer to feel good about their work, but on a practical level when they do come to revise the story it will prevent them throwing out the wrong parts when making cuts.

3. When outlining an area of the story that does not work for you, try to give plenty of detail. Sometimes it may be worth suggesting alternative wording, at other times it is as well to simply highlight passages that you found confusing, or difficult to read, and leave it to the writer to think through another way to put it.

4. Don't try to suggest style changes which make the author write in your style rather than their own. If you normally write romance and they are writing horror,

then their sentence structure and word choices may be very different from your own. Ensure the points which do not resonate with you are genuinely areas that warrant rewriting and not simply a different style to the genre you normally write in. It is not right for every story to have a happy ending for example.

5. Find a way to give feedback that works for you both. Tracked changes and comments in word processing packages can be a very efficient way to do it. However, not all packages are consistent in the way they work. Sometimes technical incompatibilities may mean you need to find another way.

6. When you are providing feedback make sure you read the piece thoroughly. Comments made on a quick skim of the work may end up being misleading. Give the work the same degree of attention that you hope others will give yours.

7. When someone goes to the trouble of providing you with feedback always remember to say thank you. Even if you don't agree with everything they have said, they have given you their time freely and you need to show appreciation of that.

8. You don't have to accept everything that someone else says about your work. However, don't simply go through dismissing the points made. Take time to mull over them and let them sink in. Try to see the particular section of the work through the reader's eyes to see if you can better understand the point being made. But, it is your story and must still reflect your style. In reworking something don't lose that vital voice that should be consistent throughout the work.

Be prepared to reciprocate. Being part of a critiquing group is a two way process. If you don't have time to give to the work of other writers, then why should they take the time with yours? You can actually learn a great deal by reading the work of another writer in this level of detail. It's surprising how often the points you pick up will resonate with things in your own writing which you might need to work on.

EXERCISE

If you're finding this book useful then leave a review on Goodreads and/or Amazon. If you aren't finding it helpful, then send us an email telling us what else you need from it.

DIFFERENT VERSIONS OF ENGLISH

PC: In theory, Australia, Canada, USA, Ireland, South Africa, New Zealand, the UK and many other countries speak and write English. In reality they use very different versions of the language. We probably all know that pants and thongs are underwear in the UK and outerwear and footwear in America and Australia respectively. I think it's also fairly common knowledge that the letter s is often replaced with a z in some countries and some omit the u after an o when spelling words such as colour and flavour. Even so, we rarely have trouble reading a different version than the one we're most familiar with.

This doesn't mean we can write in a different version. It's not as simple as checking word meanings and spellings – itself not actually a simple task as we'd need to check every single word to be absolutely sure. Sentences may be constructed differently, or tenses result in different word choices. There is also the implication behind the words to consider.

What about cultural references? You can't mention TV shows where they're not aired, or celebrities no one has heard of. Someone having private health care would be less usual in the UK than in countries without a national health service, although they may then refer to it as Health Insurance. Not everywhere has Value Added Tax (they may have Sales Tax instead), or the same system for car insurance. It's more usual for people in smaller countries to travel abroad than for those whose country is also a continent.

RJK: Attitudes to swear words vary widely too. Words considered unacceptable in the UK may be in everyday usage in Australia for example and mean something completely different to a USA reader.

It is important to remember that all language changes over time with separation. English is no different. Whilst historically in the USA they spoke English and then, as it developed American

English, the differences are in places so great that it is really a language in its own right. In part that is about simplifying the 'old' language (as we did with the languages that gave us English

> Language changes over time

originally) and partly it is about absorbing words from the other cultures that make up the Continent. English is by origin a Germanic language and if you compare many words to the German origin there are only slight variations, but we added words from French, the Scandinavian countries, Dutch and so on. It is also a living language and itself changes over time with word meanings and usage shifting.

PC: When submitting work overseas, or offering our books for sale in other countries, I think it's best to either stick to our own version of English, or to have the changes made by someone who is very familiar with the alternative version.

EXERCISE

Look at a story written by an overseas writer and set in their local area – what aspects would they need to change in order to make the story relevant to your local area?

MORE WORDS PER WEEK

101 ways to increase, and make the best use of, your writing time

1. Throw out pens which don't work first time. You could have written half a sentence each time you scribbled madly trying to get the ink to flow.
2. Don't think writing half a sentence is no help. Many would-be writers tell themselves they need several uninterrupted hours before they can write a word. Of course that helps, but it's a luxury not a necessity.
3. Writing is the thing you want to do. Don't waste your creativity coming up with excuses, use it to find the time to write. Real writers write, wannabes procrastinate.

   > Real writers write, wannabes procrastinate

4. Don't watch Eastenders. It's often harder to write when you're miserable, especially if your story is intended to end happily. Don't watch the news more than once a week. Same reason. If you want to watch a non BBC programme record it and fast forward through the adverts.
5. Don't watch something you've seen before. It's never as good the second time. Your brand new short story will be much more interesting.
6. Don't watch TV at all. Honestly, is finding out what kind of mess a bunch of celebrities make of baking, dancing or coping without their personal assistants really more important to you than your writing?
7. If you can't stop yourself watching a really gripping drama I forgive you. Just don't waste time fantasising about Aiden Turner, Benedict Cumberbatch or Holly Willoughby. Write them into your next story. Well, not them exactly; there's

libel to consider and court cases take up time and money. Just use them to get your creative juices flowing, if you know what I mean.

8. Set up your computer so your work in progress opens when you switch on and you don't go to it via Twitter, emails and Facebook.

9. Don't plagiarise, use other author's characters, breach copyright by including song lyrics, or write anything untrue about real people. I know we've said this before, but it's important! Besides, stories containing these things can't be published so you're wasting your time writing them.

10. Don't fantasise about publishers having a bidding war over your book. Instead write the story which they'll be desperate to buy.

> Stop fantasising about your completed book and start writing

11. Don't fantasise about a book signing. Write the story which will have readers queuing down the street.

12. Fantasise a lot – but always with a pen in your hand.
    RJK: Can I fantasise about cake?
    PC: Sure. It hasn't done me any harm.

13. Don't have children.
    RJK: She's joking... I hope!
    PC: Mostly. Just don't blame me if you don't get anything written until they're 27.

14. If you already have children, use them. Talking to them, or being unable to talk to them, will help you write about characters younger than yourself.

15. Don't read bought books to your children, read one of your stories (genre permitting). Reading aloud is a great way to spot typos and parts which don't flow.

16. If you write horror or erotica read it to your mother-in-law. She's already got a poor opinion of you so it can't hurt.

17. Delegate. Any able-bodied person in your home over the age of about eight is capable of helping with the housework.

18. Bringing down their own laundry isn't helping you.

Putting it in the machine along with your stuff is a start, but they're going to have to do better if they want to brag about being the child of the person who co-writes their favourite, special effects rich, epic film series.

19. Don't nag children about tidying their rooms, just tell them to keep the door shut.
20. If anyone other than you has a pet, you don't need to feed it, walk it, or clean it out unless not doing so would amount to animal cruelty.
21. Encourage children to do their homework by sitting with them and writing as they do it.
22. Don't struggle to resist buying lovely new stationery. You know you'll give in eventually so you might as well do so now. Besides, you're going to write so much more you'll need it. You'll need it all.
23. Be observant when it comes to details which will bring your story to life, but not regarding dust on your furniture and fluff on your carpets.
24. If you can afford it, consider paying someone to do your housework – but only if you can work whilst they're hoovering and you won't clean up anyway before they come.
25. Don't read bad books. Reading is important to writers, but only the good stuff. Don't waste your time on ones you're not enjoying or which are poorly written.
26. Learn shorthand (or train yourself to write slowly enough for your handwriting to be legible, or just make notes which will remind you of your great ideas).
27. Learn to type. Apparently some people can use a finger on each hand at the same time. That must speed things up! RJK: If you really struggle, try voice recognition software.
28. PC: It's drastic, but you could try getting up a bit earlier or going to bed later. Tiredness can make you less efficient though, so, contradictory as it seems, an extra hour in bed might be more helpful.
29. Don't tell people what your book will be about. Write it so you can show them.
30. Back-up your work. Rewriting lost work is a really horrible waste of time.

31. Find a writing buddy or buddies (online can work well). The encouragement and feedback will really help you produce good work.

> Team up with a writing buddy

32. Don't write something just because you think it's what people expect or because it seems fashionable at the moment. If you're not writing something which interests you, it'll be almost impossible to create something which holds the reader's attention.

33. Don't try and write like anyone else. If you copy others you're doing their work, not yours.

34. Don't hold on to knock-backs, grudges, criticisms and rejections. Dwelling on the past won't produce work which will be accepted in the future.

35. Do listen to, and use, constructive criticism to improve. Making a mistake once or twice is a learning experience. Stubbornly making it forever is a waste of time.

36. Carry a notebook and pen or pencil everywhere. Delays of any kind then become extra writing time.

37. If deadlines or goals help you get things done, set them for yourself. You could aim to meet an average daily word count, create a to do list, or commit to entering competitions.

38. Recognise all your achievements. Selling the story might be the ultimate goal, but getting the first draft done is an important step and you should stop to congratulate yourself before moving on. In the long run this is far more productive than concentrating on anything negative and losing motivation as a result.

39. Don't develop expensive tastes. Earning the money to pay for them will use up writing time.

40. Have a plan for longer pieces of writing so you don't get bogged down or sidetracked (it doesn't need to be detailed – just a few notes to keep you on course will help).

41. Don't put off things such as tax returns, getting the car's MOT or renewing your passport. Missing such deadlines wastes a lot more time than you kid yourself you're saving by not doing it when it's due.

42. Don't ignore a niggling tooth, medical symptoms or the possibility of depression. See a professional before the problem gets worse. If it turns out to be nothing serious you weren't wasting your time as you'll now be able to stop worrying about it and concentrate on your writing.

43. Don't waste time worrying what might go wrong in your life. Instead write a story where your heroine solves her problems.

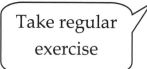
Take regular exercise

44. You need exercise. Take a plot problem with you and work out the answer as you walk/run/pole dance/swim.

45. Recognise that some of your reasons for not writing are really excuses. Trying to write invites failure, not trying guarantees it.

46. Your writing time is as important as your loved ones' interests. Remind yourself, and them, of that fact.

47. Set aside a given period (or periods) as your writing time each week and let those around you know you're unavailable. Leave the house if that's the only way to get some peace.

48. Switch your phone to silent before writing. Telling people you're not interested in PPI claims won't get the chapter finished.

49. Disconnect from the internet before writing. Yes, you might need to look something up, but you can do that later.

50. Don't buy clothes which need ironing or hand washing.

51. If you already have clothes in the house which need ironing or hand washing (by you) give them to a charity shop.

52. Give everyone you know book tokens at every gift giving 'opportunity'. (They can buy my books if yours aren't available yet.) If they don't read, phone McDonalds and ask if they sell gift vouchers.

53. Write in your lunch breaks at work

54. Write in your tea breaks (at home or work).

55. Don't neglect relationships. You'll want family and friends to help celebrate that brilliant book deal and look proud when you collect awards. Besides, divorces can take up a lot of valuable writing time.

56. Stop work every now and then. Stretch your back, shake your arms, drink a glass of water and look at something other than the screen or notebook. Aches, stiffness and dehydration are no help to a writer.

57. If you regularly drink a lot of alcohol, cut back. Hangovers don't help with writing.

58. Don't keep reworking old stories which never sold. Write something new instead.

> Don't spend too long reworking – write something new

59. Ignore anyone who says you shouldn't be writing or otherwise puts you down. The time wasted listening to them would be better used writing that prize winning piece which will prove them wrong.

60. Re-calibrate all your clocks so you get 25 hours every day. Or, more realistically, allocate a little less time to all the other things you want, or have to do. Wash your hair, but don't straighten it. Mow the lawn but don't deadhead the lobelia. Make a hearty family meal, but serve fruit for dessert. You get the idea.

61. Learn to recognise when you're wasting time. If what you're doing isn't necessary or fun then maybe it's a time wasting habit you should try to stop.

62. Join a writing group. Take classes, attend workshops. The information and encouragement you receive should more than make up for the hours you're there.

> It's ok to take a break

63. Maintain a balance. If you really don't feel like writing, or other things genuinely are more important at the moment then it's O.K. to take a break.

64. Taking a break from writing is not the same as giving up. When the situation changes, get writing again.

65. Consider techniques such as 'morning pages' or short meditations before writing sessions to see if they help you be more productive, but don't continue if they don't work

for you.

66. Don't measure your progress or results against others. If you've done a good day's work for you, then you've done a good day's work regardless of whether it's more or less than someone else's output.

67. Emails arrive instantly, but that doesn't mean you must read and respond instantly. Would you do the same if it had come by post? Set your computer to only download them once an hour at the most. When you do read them, delete anything unimportant straight away.

68. Don't just sit there trying to find the perfect word – get the story down and polish it later.

69. Say no. You don't have to accept every party invitation, attend every event at the social club, always go for a pint with the lads after work. Spending time with friends is important, but then so is your writing. Do the things you really want to, but don't get stuck in time wasting habits which are no fun.

70. Keep saying no. If friends and family are experiencing real problems then of course you'll want to help, but you don't always need to give up six hours just to make their day a little easier. Their wants aren't more important than yours.

71. Say yes. If anyone offers to do something which will save you time or make your life easier, or help you research your book, then enthusiastically accept. Just remember to return the favour, or name them on the dedication page.

72. Consider a recording or dictation device so you can write whilst you're doing other things.

73. Keep frozen pizza in the freezer. If you don't want to cook, heating one of those is much quicker (and cheaper) than going out to dinner, or fetching a take away. Using the box it came in as a serving tray saves washing plates, but drinking from the bottle is a step too far.

74. If you cook proper meals yourself, do double quantities and freeze half. Teach someone else how to warm it up.

75. If you have a book out, don't check your Amazon rankings every three minutes. Don't check your friends'/rivals'/ enemies' rankings either.

76. Don't wait. Not for feedback, competition results, requests

for the rest of the manuscript or to hear if work has been accepted. Get on with writing something else. If it's a 'no' you'll have something else to try. If it's a 'yes' they might want more from you.

77. Don't wait for anything. Write instead. You can write until your hair stylist is free, when the train is delayed and while your friend chats to someone else on her phone. (If she keeps doing that stay at home writing instead of going out with her.)

> Don't wait for a response before writing the next story

78. If you feel blocked or uninspired, you can still make use of your time. Try researching markets, proof reading something you finished recently, updating your accounts, visiting friends' blogs to offer encouragement, or sharpening all your pencils.

79. Ideally find a potential market before you start writing. No point writing a 15,000 word story on an obscure theme which has no possible home.

80. Stop tweaking! Try to recognise when you're changing, but not improving, the story.

81. Subscribe to any magazines you use for help or research – newsagents are far too distracting.

82. Use lots of very short words! That might sound like a joke, but I'm partly serious. Often the shortest, most obvious, word really is best. 'Tea' will generally be better than 'beverage', 'car' an improvement on 'vehicle' and 'mobile phone' preferably to 'mobile telecommunications device'.

83. Only use words you're confident you know the meaning of and which you can spell.

84. Learn the meaning and spelling of lots of words, so you're always able to use the one which best expresses your meaning.

85. Eat raw fruits and vegetables, but not only those. That would save time, but it's possible to take things too far. A healthy diet helps towards a healthy body, which makes everything, including writing, easier.

86. If you are ill or injured write anyway. Stephen King did it

with a broken back, Stephen Hawking can't find it easy to write his books, Charles Dickens suffered 'peculiar and troubling' symptoms for the last five years of his life, yet continued to work.

87. Shop somewhere such as Aldi or Lidl. Smaller shop sizes and product ranges make it a quicker job than is the case with huge supermarkets.

RJK: Or shop online.

> ## Use research more than once

88. PC: Use research more than once. Specialising in one non-fiction field, setting several historical stories in the same time period, or re-using a location means your work does double duty.

89. Consider writing a series. Starting with characters and a world you know well, can save time.

90. Don't try to do it all. Better to finish one piece than write half a book, a few notes for an article, two scenes of a play and a few verses of a poem before abandoning them all and starting a short story.

91. Unless you're the driver, write on the journey to work/college/anywhere else.

92. If you are the driver consider switching to public transport or car sharing (it's better for the environment too).

93. Buy copies of this book for all your writing friends and leave us a 5 star review. This guarantees an extra hour's writing time per day.

RJK: But only if you're living in a fantasy world!
PC: Oh. O.K. then. I confess this may not actually work.

94. Don't waste time disagreeing with your editor when you know she's right.

RJK: Which according to my husband is most of the time!

95. PC: Keep fiction for the page. It's hard work maintaining a lie and time consuming sorting out the mess when you're found out.

96. If you must stray from the straight and narrow do something which will earn you a long stretch. You'll get lots of writing time in prison and, annoyingly and unfairly,

the notoriety will help your career.

97. Don't let things such as 'building a platform' take up so much time you've nothing to launch from it. But do make a start if you feel you'll need it in the future.

98. Do offer your time and support to writing friends. Their work is important too and you know they'll be there when you need them.

99. Edit your stories. Totally rewrite them if they need it. Proofread carefully. These things use time, they don't waste it.

> Don't sit there, write something!

100. Try word sprints. Set a timer for ten minutes and write as much as possible.

101. Don't sit there marvelling at my brilliant advice – go write something!

EXERCISE

Action one or more of the above and use the time for writing.

SECTION 4

WHAT TO DO WITH YOUR WORK

WOMAG FICTION

What is womag fiction?

To state the (almost) obvious, Womag stories, or women's magazine fiction, are short stories in a distinct style, aimed at a particular market – women's magazines.

Or to be less obvious, but more accurate, it's a range of fiction lengths, aimed at a variety of markets, each with its own requirements which differ slightly. There's a range of styles and genres too, or perhaps sub genres. All submissions do need to be stories though. Scenes, anecdotes, jokes, essays and anything which isn't a story won't do.

Women's magazines provide one of the biggest and most accessible markets for short stories.

Many of the rules which apply to writing in general, and to other short stories also apply to writing womag stories.

In addition, they also have their own particular rules. Some apply to individual magazines and some to the genre as a whole.

Guidelines

Almost all the women's magazines produce detailed submission guidelines. Often they can be found online. In some cases, you may need to request them in writing. Guidelines, or links to them, can be found on www.womagwriter.blogspot.co.uk.

Always read the guidelines

If guidelines are unavailable, this is usually a sign that unsolicited submissions are not considered.

Failing to obtain and follow the latest version will seriously reduce your chances of success. My advice is general, whilst in the guidelines it is specific and regularly updated. If there's a conflict between the two, always follow the guidelines when submitting to that particular magazine.

Guidelines give information on the type of story the editor is looking for, the word counts needed and instructions on how to submit your stories. If there are subjects or genres they particularly do, or do not, wish to see this will be mentioned; as will any peculiarities with regard to formatting. They'll also give an idea of how long you should expect to wait for a reply.

Once you're considered a regular contributor you may receive further guidance in the form of emailed newsletters.

Which women's magazines publish fiction?

At the time of writing (autumn 2016) the following UK magazines accept unsolicited fiction, that means anyone at all may send in their work.

Take a Break's Fiction Feast (TABFF)

This is a monthly publication with twenty stories of varying lengths per issue. (700 and 1,200 word stories are most in demand.) There is also a weekly magazine, which doesn't currently carry fiction. A variety of specials exist, including seasonal ones and *Fate and Fortune*. These sometimes include a one page story. Any submissions sent will be considered for both *Fiction Feast* and the specials.

Twist ending stories are popular as are ghost stories, crime, spine chillers, romance, family sagas and humour. Whilst historical or nostalgic stories are unlikely to find favour, you may get success with tales which have genuinely creepy or alarming moments. Characters may be flawed and will face real problems which are taboo in other publications. These can include illness, unemployment, disability, domestic violence or loneliness. Not all stories end happily ever after, but they all have an upbeat or positive ending.

Most stories have women as the main characters, but tales told from the point of view of a man or child are also featured.

Readers are most likely to be women aged 25-55 with children.

Submit by post, with an sae for the reply.
Norah McGrath (Fiction Editor), Take a Break, 24-28 Oval Road,
London, NW1 7DT.

You are requested to include a short summary (two or three lines)
which should appear under the title.

The Weekly News (TWN)

This weekly publication looks like a newspaper and can be hard
to track down. Usually two single page stories (1,200 to 1,500
words) are published per issue, but occasionally an issue will
feature six stories including a couple of longer ones.

Twist endings, crime, and ghost stories are popular, but the
variety of genres and themes is huge. Themes which aren't
generally considered women's interest such as war or sports
related stories might find a home here, as might romance or those
involving family relationships.

Male characters and/or a male point of view are as welcome as
female. Third person past tense is preferred. Jill Finlay, the fiction
editor, often makes decisions quite close to the publication date,
so seasonal stories can be submitted later than for other
magazines.

Readers are mainly over 50. A third of them are male (a much
higher percentage than for most other magazines).

Submit (one story at a time) by email to jfinlay@dcthomson.co.uk
You should get an automatic acknowledgement. If the story has
not been accepted within three months, Jill Finlay says, 'this
indicates that your story has not been selected for publication and
you're free submit elsewhere'.

Woman's Weekly (WW) and Woman's Weekly Fiction Special (WWFS).

The weekly magazine usually has two short stories. There will
also be an instalment of a serial. For these it's best to contact the

editor at the planning stage to be sure the subject is something they'd consider and not similar to something already in the pipeline. The fiction special is monthly and carries twenty stories per issue. These range from one to eight pages. (1,000 to 8,000 words)

Ghost stories, twist endings, crime, spine chillers, romance, family sagas and humour are all popular. These may be contemporary, nostalgic or historical. Stories are often emotional and may be very sad in places, but will always have an uplifting ending. Science fiction is not wanted.

The editor likes different formats, such as stories written as letters or texts, divided up by days of the week, seasons, or letters of the alphabet. Multiple points of view are also acceptable. All these devices must add to the story though and not simply be gimmicks.

Readers are of a wide age range, but generally female with children or grandchildren. Bear in mind they receive around 350 submissions each week.

All work submitted is considered for the whole range.

Submit by post, including an sae, until you have a story accepted. Once your work has been accepted submissions and responses may be emailed. The fiction editor is Gaynor Davies.

Fiction Department, Woman's Weekly, Time Inc. (UK), Blue Fin Building, 110 Southwark Street, London, SE1 0SU.

The People's Friend (TPF)

This is another weekly publication with several short stories per issue. They also publish serials and 10,000 word crime stories. A variety of specials also carry fiction.

Popular genres are romance, humour, nostalgia, family and historical. They are very unlikely to take ghost stories and aren't keen on twist endings. More focus should be on the characters than the plot. This is one of the longest running UK magazines and is still very traditional.

Stories are quite gentle with no shocks. Stories which feature anything upsetting such as illness, divorce, death or unkindness are unlikely to be accepted even with a happy ending. That can make creating enough conflict a challenge, but this is still needed. Characters should be 'ordinary' of any age, male or female.

RJK: What is meant by 'ordinary'?

PC: They don't actually say, but I believe they mean people who have (or had) jobs to pay the rent, rather than footballer's wives and royalty.

Readers are adult, likely to have grandchildren, be family orientated and with traditional views. There's a big age range but they're mostly retired. Although there are more male readers than for many other magazines, it's still a mainly female readership.

The People's Friend will also consider unsolicited non-fiction articles and poetry. For more information, it is worth reading their blog as well as the website.

Submit by post. There is an editorial team, any of whom may respond. Once work has been accepted you will generally deal with the same editor from then on. You may request that your replies are emailed, which avoids having to supply an sae.

The People's Friend, D.C. Thomson & Co., Ltd., 80 Kingsway East, Dundee, DD4 8SL.

Yours

This is a fortnightly publication with a single one page story per issue. (1,000 to 1,200 words)

Favoured themes include romance, families, grandchildren, nostalgia and wartime comradeship. Anything downbeat such as death, widowhood, illness or loneliness should be avoided as story themes.

Yours will also consider unsolicited non-fiction articles.

Readers are most likely to be retired and female.

Submit by post. Short Stories, Yours Magazine, Bauer Media, Media House, Peterborough Business Park, Peterborough, PE2 6EA.

Or by email to yours@bauermedia.co.uk

In both cases include a synopsis of 100 to 150 words

This magazine accepts work only on an all rights basis (for this reason I don't submit to them). Please see the copyright section if you're unsure what this means.

Prima

This is a monthly magazine with a single one page story per issue. (Usually they ask that these are under 800 words.) It's actually a competition, but there's no practical difference between entering this and submitting elsewhere.

Stories tend to be fairly simple and linear in style. First or third person may be used. They often read as though they may be true (perhaps some are). Themes include romance, work and family relationships.

Readers are mainly female, aged 30 – 55 with children.

Submit my email, attaching a head and shoulders photo of yourself. This will be published with your story, should you win. yourwinningstory@hearst.co.uk

---

Other UK magazines which publish fiction, but don't currently accept unsolicited material are:

Candis

This magazine is published monthly, with one story per issue. All fiction is now commissioned.

that's life!

There's no fiction in the weekly magazine. Occasionally a commissioned story appears in a seasonal special.

My Weekly (MW)

This weekly magazine, and its various specials, publishes quite a lot of fiction, including serials, but you may only submit if you're 'known' to them. If you've sold fiction to them before, even if it was quite a while ago, you may submit stating this fact. Your short fiction will also be considered if you manage to sell them a feature or a pocket novel. They accept unsolicited submissions for both of those.

Overseas magazines which accept unsolicited fiction are:

Allas

This is a weekly Swedish publication, with several stories per issue. (Their length requirements are stated in character counts not words and this is calculated on the Swedish version. Good luck with that!) They also print serials. It's published in Swedish, but submissions are accepted in English and if your covering letter is written in English your replies will be in that language too (A much better version of it than my attempts at Swedish!)

Stories are upbeat and exciting, funny or emotional. Romance and family relationships are popular. Violence isn't welcome, but there is a regular crime slot.

Most readers are female and aged from 20 – 45.

Submit by email to lotta.gustavsson@allas.aller.se

that's life! and that's life! Fast Fiction

There is a weekly version of this Australian magazine with a one page story (700 words) per issue as well as the quarterly *Fast Fiction*. This is similar to *TABFF* and accepts stories in a range of lengths (600 to 1,800 words). Suitable submissions are considered for both publications.

Seasonal stories are popular with this publication. Christmas, Hallowe'en and Easter as well as Anzac Day and Melbourne Cup Day. Remember the Australian winter coincides with our summer.

Other welcome themes are romance, ghost stories, thrillers and humour.

Readers are mainly aged 25 to 55 and female.

Submit by email, stating story title, word count and genre in the subject line. fastfiction@pacificmags.com.au

The fiction editor is Judie Durrant.

You

This is a weekly South African magazine published in English.

Any genre is considered. Romance, twist endings and whodunnits are the most popular. Stories should be contemporary, not 'too high-brow or morbid'. (Word count required is around 1,500 words.)

You is considered a family magazine with readers from young adult upwards. They may be male or female.

Submit by post or email. stories@you.co.za
Fiction Editor (Lynn Ely) PO Box 7167, Roggebaai 8012, South Africa.

Ireland's Own

There's enough of a clue in the title for you to work out where this weekly magazine is based. Each issue has several short stories of approximately 2,000 words, as do lots of different specials so there are plenty of opportunities. *Ireland's Own* is often available in large UK newsagents.

This magazine is very traditional in tone and appearance, rather like an Irish version of *TPF*. Popular topics are nostalgia, romance, family stories and humour. They prefer stories told in a straightforward, linear manner.

Readers are generally retired and may be men or women.

Non-fiction articles are also considered.

Submit by email. submissions@irelandsown.ie

Woman's Era

This fortnightly publication is based in India. (I know of several people outside of India who've had work published, but don't know of any who've received their payment.)

The magazine is published in English and has several stories per issue. A range of genres are accepted, although romance seems particularly popular.

Readers are female and aged 20 upwards.

Submit by post or email newmedia@womansera.com
Mr. Divesh Nath, Editor, Woman's Era, E 3 Jhandewalan Estate, Rani Jhansi Road, New Delhi 110055, India.

Woman's World

This American magazine is published weekly.

They use only two genres; true to life romance and 'solve it yourself' mysteries. They like engaging, down-to-earth characters and a brisk plot.

Readers are female and aged 30 to 55.

Submit by email to fiction@womansworldmag.com

Overseas magazines which publish fiction, but have restrictions about who may submit are:

Hjemmet

There are versions of this magazine in Norway, Sweden and Denmark. Unsolicited submissions are not welcomed. You would need to be VAT registered in order to be published with them!

Yours

This is a fortnightly Australian magazine for female readers over 50. Unsolicited submissions are not welcomed.

Take 5

A weekly Australian magazine. Readers are female, young adult and upwards.

This is a sister publication to *Take a Break* and often uses stories previously published in the UK. Under the terms of the *TAB* contract they can do this without paying the author an additional fee.

If you have a story you think is particularly suitable for this market, then it may still be worth submitting directly – particularly if you're Australian. (Word count range approx. 600 to 2,700.)

Submit by email take5@bauer-media.com.au

Rights taken

The rights required by the various magazines vary considerably and are subject to change. Because of this, ALWAYS read the current guidelines and any contract or agreement carefully and follow them. You could be in legal trouble if you fail to do this.

As a guide, most womags require stories which have never been published anywhere before, (although some may consider stories which were published in another language). Publishing on your own blog, or in open forums would normally be considered 'published' by womags. They won't want to offer for sale something which is available free elsewhere. Don't forget that caching means work might still be visible even after you've deleted it.

> Most womags want unpublished stories

Don't be tempted to change the title and character names and submit a previously published story somewhere which doesn't allow this. The fee won't cover your legal costs for breach of contract and neither publisher will accept anything from you again.

You may be able to sell reprints to a few publications, but check contracts and guidelines of both magazines.

Most magazines require exclusive use for a period (which can vary from three to eighteen months) and non-exclusive use thereafter. Normally they require print and electronic rights, some want audio too.

Usually after a stated period has passed, you will be permitted to re-use the work in your own collection, offer them to an anthology or enter them in some competitions. Note: this is not always the case! If you give up your copyright, it is gone forever. (See section on copyright.)

Overseas publications

For publications in languages other than English, you won't be required to translate your words, but you might like to do a little translation of stories for overseas markets.

> You are not required to translate

Character names are an obvious thing to change. Just as with UK names, you can do an internet search to find out which were most popular baby names for each year and therefore pick something to suit your character's age.

Place names will also need to be changed. Don't forget to take distances into account and I'm not just thinking of changing miles to kilometres. For example, a character living in London could travel to Paris and back in a day, if he needed to. Or perhaps go there for a weekend break. Setting that same story in Australia would require a little more work than deleting London, France and Paris, and inserting Canberra, New Zealand and Wellington.

The weather, brand names and customs will be different. Readers might be far more concerned about finding a big hairy spider than they would in the UK. Don't get caught out by having your back to school stories set in September or Mother's Day in March as they would be in the UK.

I won't go on; you've got the message.

How short are they?

Requirements vary with each magazine. They also change fairly frequently. Because of this, please always check the current guidelines (O.K. I might go on about that, but it is VERY important). Overall the range is from around 600 to 10,000 words. That doesn't mean any word count within those limits is acceptable. Generally, stories will cover one or more whole pages, so editors will require a word count which can easily be accommodated.

> The number of words to a page varies between titles

Just to further muddy the waters, there isn't any consistency over the number of words per page. With *TABFF* the ideal word count for a single page is 700, with *WW* it's 900 to 1,000 and with *TWN* it's 1,200 to 1,500. That means a story perfect in length for one, simply can't be used by another; at least not without considerable changes by the author prior to submission.

Once over 2,000 words, the precise length is usually less important. That's because things such as illustrations and adverts can occupy some of the space.

With some magazines, there's also the possibility of selling serials in three, four or five parts. The stories will need to be of a similar style to one off shorts, but of course more complex and all, except for the final part, must end on a cliffhanger. *My Weekly*, *WW*, *Allas* and *TPF* all publish serials. Payment for each serial instalment is generally as high, or higher, than that offered for a single story. Talking of payments, they vary from magazine to magazine too. Often word count will make a difference, as will exchange rates for overseas sales. Sometimes the author's experience is also a factor. The range is from about £45 to £500.

Pocket novels are another option. These are published separately from the magazines for a one off fee (which is no more than some publications pay for a single short story, but it is sometimes possible to earn Public Lending Rights (PLR) or sell large print rights). For *My Weekly* they're around 50,000 words. *TPF* only require 42,000. They are usually romances; contemporary, nostalgic or historical.

For a one page story you'll require a fairly simple framework. Probably just one major incident and one or two characters. That doesn't mean they must be lightweight, although they might be. Very short stories can be highly emotional and/or cover big, important themes. Twist ending stories generally work best as short pieces.

The way I fit my story to the guidelines is to write the first draft, then decide which magazine I feel it's most suitable for and check their word count requirements. I then compare the guidelines with the figure for my draft and adjust accordingly during the rewrite. That's the theory anyway!

What are the genres?

Stories can be in almost any genre, as long as the guidelines don't state otherwise. They will have to be an appropriate version of that genre though. A womag version of a horror story or erotica would need to be very mild. A bit scary in places, or sensual rather than sexy. Twist endings are popular, but they need to be 'proper' stories as well as have a twist.

Not all stories need a happy ever after ending, but almost all will end on a positive

> Not all stories need a happy ending

or uplifting note. These stories are for entertainment. If you wish to raise issues which are important to you, then do it with a light touch.

Which writing rules apply to womag stories?

Stories should follow all normal short story rules (and break them at times too). One which applies particularly

> Arrive late, leave early

is - 'arrive late, leave early'. This means that you avoid any build up to the story and dive right into the action. Stop writing the moment the conflict has been resolved or the twist revealed. Think of it as having Sunday lunch out. Would you get to the pub at nine to watch them peel the potatoes or hang around to supervise the washing up once you'd eaten? Readers of womag stories generally either have little time (they might be reading in a coffee break at work) or are likely to have distractions, such as children to care for. You need to grab their attention quickly, but not keep them longer than necessary.

Don't have too many characters and choose those characters wisely. Readers will need to identify with them or care about them. One way to aid empathy is to have them the same age, sex, financial status etc., as the reader, as long as that fits with the story. Another is to have them experience the same issues your reader might face. Knowing these things about your readers forms a vital part of your research.

We don't only care about people like us though; many of us are naturally a little protective of children, and anyone vulnerable. We like nice people, but can care about nasty ones too, we'll want them to get their comeuppance, or learn the error of their ways.

Have the character solve their own problems, or at least help with the resolution.

Try to avoid 'white space' stories; those which don't seem to be set anywhere. Simply mentioning the kitchen floor, bedroom window or supermarket till will fix that.

Dialogue

Use lots of dialogue

Lots of dialogue is good. You can start with it. Use plenty of tags so it's clear who is talking. Remember these stories are supposed to be a quite easy read and no one will want to puzzle over your meaning. Some magazines insist on every piece of dialogue being attributed, even when only two people are speaking.

You can also vary 'he said' with info giving tags, such as 'George sighed'. This is useful with such a small word count and allows us to very simply say what we might otherwise show in a different way, if we had space to do that. Don't get carried away though and have people expostulating, snickering and twittering when really they're speaking quite normally.

SPAG

It's unlikely your story will be rejected for a typo, but Spelling, Punctuation and Grammar should be as close to perfect as possible. Getting these things right makes the editor's life easier. You want that! It makes things easier for the reader too. One of the distinguishing features of womag fiction is that it's easy to read.

There's a myth that colons and semi colons are outlawed in womag fiction. They aren't, but they should only be used where necessary. If splitting into two sentences, or substituting a comma would retain the meaning, then do that. If you don't, it's likely the editor will.

Correct is one thing, complicated is another. Generally, use short, simple sentences, with easy to follow constructions. Write in an informal style. Keep tenses simple – past, present and future are usually all you'll need.

> Short simple sentences

Sentence fragments and ellipses are fine, especially in dialogue.

Who should write womag stories?

Pretty much anyone who can write can have a go. It doesn't matter if you're male or female. Although you'll need to give your real name for the signing of contracts and getting paid, the story may be published under a pen name if you wish.

Your age, ethnic background, sexual orientation, previous writing history, etc., don't matter and there's no reason to give this information. All the editor is concerned about is whether she feels her readers will enjoy that particular story and if it will fit into the magazine.

> Read the publications first

It will help if you read and enjoy the stories in the publication you intend to submit to.

Who shouldn't write womag stories?

Anyone who strongly dislikes women's magazine fiction or feels it is inferior to 'proper' writing. If you consider womag stories are too lightweight, unrealistic etc., then don't submit.

Working on stories you don't enjoy is no fun and you're unlikely to do it well. Why would you want to be associated with what you consider rubbish anyway?

Can the rules be broken?

Of course!

That is, they sometimes can, if that's done with caution. But only some rules and you're lowering your chances of success if you don't follow the current guidelines. If you genuinely feel your story will suit the magazine, even if it appears to push the boundaries a little, then send it in.

> Be careful how you break the rules

If you want to write something very different from the usual womag stories then write them, but find another market to submit them to.

How do I decide what to write about?

Research is the answer. Luckily it's the fun kind.

Read the magazines, both to get a feel for the type of thing they want and to see what they never include. Is the omission a gap in the market or something they don't want? Also see what they've used recently. Don't make yours too similar; maybe change the story location, or job of the main character if these featured in a previous story. Don't rely on old copies for research. Things change.

Look at the letters pages, adverts, features and articles to see what interests the readers. Magazines often have social media accounts. Following helps you get a better feel for what they and their readers want. You can also look at the information provided to advertisers. This will usually give details of the readers' age range, social class and interests.

If you're in the target group, write a list of your interests, jobs you've done, hobbies, things you've chosen to read about or watch TV programmes on, ways you've spent your time in the past week. All these will make suitable story topics.

I know I've mentioned this before, but always check the current guidelines. These can be very detailed in terms of what they do and don't want.

How do I submit?

In accordance with the current guidelines! But, if they don't state to the contrary then…

> **Send only what you're asked for**

Don't submit more than you need to. You generally don't need to explain the story or provide a synopsis and, unless you're asked to do so, it's better not to and let the story speak for itself. The editor doesn't care about your writing history, qualifications, motivation or that your mum loves this story. They just care about this particular story, so that's really all they need to see.

The editor will need to know your name, pen name if you use one, your contact details, story title and word count. They may also need to know if the story is seasonal or otherwise time sensitive and if it's aimed at a particular slot. Usually magazines buy first rights, but if something else is being offered you may wish to clarify that too.

If emailing, then the body of the email acts as your covering letter and will include all the above information. The story is simply attached. When posting, you generally have the choice of a covering letter, a title page, or simply putting your name and contact details on the story document. Don't do all of these. It just wastes everyone's time.

Submit as requested. If they say email only, don't pop round with your handwritten story.

Use a big enough envelope so that your story isn't a crumpled mess. A paperclip holding it together is appreciated by some editors. Don't use unnecessary packaging, folders, bindings etc.

Ensure return envelopes are properly addressed and have the correct postage.

Generally, you can have more than one story 'out' with a magazine at the same time, but sending more than they can use means you're just competing against yourself. If multiple submissions are O.K., then it'll make things easier all round if you use separate emails for each story.

It's better to wait for a response from the first few submissions before sending more. Perhaps they'll mention an error you can correct in the others, or they might give useful feedback you'll be able to take into account.

Formatting

The standard layout is to:

Use white A4 paper. Your computer's default settings will be fine for margins. Double line space the entire document. Indent paragraphs rather than leaving a gap between them. Only print on one side of the paper.

Use a clear, modern print, no fancy fonts or colours and no illustrations. Number pages – and it's a good idea to have author name and story title in the headers or footers too.

> Use a clear modern font

Some editors have particular requirements on formatting, if so, these will be in the guidelines. Always follow these even if they seem contrary to standard practice. For example *TPF* don't like paragraphs to be indented.

Don't get too concerned about all this. Anything important will be mentioned in the guidelines. As long as you follow these and the editor can actually read your story, minor formatting issues are unlikely to get your story rejected. Neither will beautiful formatting make up for deficiencies in the plot.

Sometimes once a story is accepted you'll be asked to reformat it to the editor's requirements. In the case of *TAB* you'll be asked to remove tabs or indents and to ensure all speech quotes are the single kind. Make sure you do this, even if you have to ask a more technically minded friend for help.

Seasonal stories

Seasonal stories need to be submitted well in advance, up to six months in some cases. That doesn't mean you can't write a Christmas story on Boxing Day, or beach stories as you sunbathe, if that's when inspiration strikes and time allows. I often do this myself as it's easier to get into the right mood and to capture the little details which bring a story to life. For me, that more than makes up for the delay before I can submit them.

> Submit seasonal stories well in advance

Be wary of topical subjects. Will they still be of interest once the story is in print? If it's rejected the first time, will you have another chance to sell it?

Contracts and guidelines

Almost all the magazines will require you to sign a contract before your work will be published and it's extremely unlikely you'll be able to negotiate anything other than the standard terms. Standard for that publication I mean, as they're all different. Read any contracts and be sure you understand, BEFORE signing. Keep a copy and stick to it once you have signed.

Dealing with editors

If they say no, accept it. Replying to your complaint will take up the time they could have spent reading your future submissions, as well as causing irritation.

You don't have a right to feedback, or anything else, simply because you tried to sell them something. Yes, they do need our stories – but you've chosen to send, they haven't asked you to (unless they have asked us – in that case, you should expect a reply of some kind). If you do get any feedback that's often a really good sign, even if it does seem negative. It takes time to do this, so an editor will only bother if your work shows promise.

If asked to make changes, then do it! Yes, even if you don't

> **If asked to make changes, do it!**

agree with their suggestions. It's a really useful exercise. Keep your original version, so if after following their request you don't like it, you still have a version you are happy with. If you still don't agree then you don't have to resubmit, but having tried will make you better able to write to their requirements in future.

Don't feel you have to rush to do it immediately (unless they've stressed a quick response is needed). Think it through, make the changes and leave it for a while, get feedback, just as you would with a new story.

Editors may make changes without consulting you. Often titles are changed to fit house style, or because they've been used before. Character names might be changed, especially if they're the same as for other stories in the magazine. Words

> **Title may be changed before publication**

may be cut or added to help with the layout. Just accept all of these. Sometimes they'll make changes you feel are wrong or weaken the story. Perhaps they'll simplify punctuation or grammar, even add the 'he expostulated' type speech tags. Live with it.

Sometimes bigger changes will be made. Usually they'll either ask you to make these, or discuss them with you, but not always. Live with it. Basically if you sell it, the story is no longer yours and they can do what they like with it. You may have retained some rights (and I do hope you have) but that particular version has still been sold. You wouldn't sell your house then go back later and complain you didn't like the new wallpaper... would you?

Hopefully editors will fix your typos and other errors. Be grateful if they do, but they may still slip through. Don't blame them for not spotting a mistake you missed.

Don't swamp editors. If they publish one story a month, there's no point sending three a week.

Other womag writing?

Many magazines publish readers' letters, tips, jokes and funny photos. These are sometimes referred to as 'fillers'. Submitting these helps research the market, boosts your confidence and possibly bank balance too.

Several magazines accept unsolicited non-fiction articles, or nostalgia pieces. Others will consider pitches for these and might commission work if your idea is original and you can convince the editor you're in a good position to write the piece.

Tips for success

Concentrate on one market at a time (even if you do send stuff elsewhere). Read several issues and try to write more than one story for them. Don't give up just because you've had several rejections from one market. As long as you're sending suitable work

> Concentrate on one market at a time

and not too much of it, previous rejections don't count against you. Failing to heed advice will though. As will repeatedly ignoring the guidelines.

Get lots out there. In part it's a numbers game.

Don't forget to claim ALCS on all stories published in UK magazines (see glossary).

Support the magazines by subscribing. As a reader let them know you enjoy fiction, perhaps by composing a letter to the editor, or mentioning on social media a story you particularly enjoyed.

Most themes have already been used, so try an unusual approach. Maybe you'll choose a less obvious character. For example, how does a divorce affect an employee or neighbour? What about a first date perhaps told through the eyes of the waiter, or couple on the next table? Could you use a different time period or an unexpected location? Maybe you'll focus on one tiny detail rather than tell the bigger story.

Most importantly, tell the most interesting story you can and write it to the best of your ability. So really, the 'secret' to succeeding with womags is the same as with all other writing.

EXERCISE

Study one of the women's magazines and plan a story which you think would be a good fit. Ideally, write the story and send a submission.

101 COMPETITION POINTERS

1. Some competitions launch writing careers, or provide enough money to, at least temporarily, give up the day job and concentrate on writing.
2. Any hint of success will boost a writer's belief in their work and encourage them to keep going.
3. Wins and shortlist mentions help build an online presence and raise your profile – this can be helpful in attracting publishers or marketing existing work.
4. Leaping around in excitement on hearing the good news will burn off a few calories.
5. Winning stories are often published.
6. Winners are frequently invited to submit a short biography, which can be an excellent promotion tool.
7. The prestige of winning can help you earn paid work. (*Writing Magazine* bought my article on this subject. Would they have done if I hadn't picked up at least a few prizes?)
8. Winning doesn't have to be the end. Sometimes stories can win more than one prize, or perhaps you'll publish a collection of prize winners.
9. Be proud of success. Publicity and kudos are part of the prize so make the most of it. When appropriate, mention wins to editors, publishers, those who hire speakers for events.

    Read writing magazines

10. But first, catch your competition. Read adverts in writing magazines, competition supplements, newsletters and forums.
11. Check local papers and magazines, in libraries, on company websites, even junk mail.
12. Get yourself on mailing lists. As well as competition organisers, writing related sites and businesses send out

details of competitions.

13. Visit www.patsy-collins.blogspot.com for free entry competitions. Facebook and Twitter are good too if you follow the right people and organisations.

14. Join writing groups, both in person and online to share competition news.

15. Don't just try for cash prizes. Some competitions offer things money can't buy – to meet a writing hero, publishing deals, or to have your work performed.

16. Make sure you want, and can accept, the prize. If it's a place on a course or event which you can't attend, is it fair to enter? Do you have room for a lifetime supply of banana scented toilet cleaner?

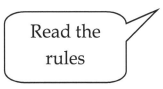

Read the rules

17. Read the rules.

18. Now read them again slowly while paying attention! At first glance they often seem similar and it's easy to assume they're all pretty much the same. They aren't.

19. Don't be tempted to cheat in any way. You're likely to be rumbled and then agents, publishers and editors will be wary of dealing with you.

20. Unless you have lots of spare money, set yourself a budget for competition entries, printing and postage. If you're lucky enough to win a cash prize you could add that back into the pot.

21. Look at the prize in relation to the entry fee. A £35 fee with nothing but a pretty certificate to reward the winner might not be a good investment – although the chances of winning should be high.

22. Entry fees sometimes include feedback, or this can be obtained for a small extra fee. That's valuable if the competition is a regular one or the feedback reveals a weakness you were unaware of.

Watch out for scams

23. Most competitions are perfectly genuine, but there are a few scams. It might be worth doing an internet search to see if anyone has made complaints.

24. Follow the rules.

25. Follow ALL the rules. I judged a small competition in which over half the entrants disqualified themselves by not doing so. The most common error was with formatting. It might appear trivial, but it didn't seem fair to award the prize to someone who'd broken the rules, no matter how excellent their entry. Unlike general submissions, competition judges are unlikely to be able to offer flexibility if requirements have not been met precisely as it would be unfair to those entrants who have taken the time to follow them to the letter.

26. If you don't understand a rule, ask. Not your mum, mate in the writing group or the tea leaves. Ask the organisers.

27. If you're a beginner writer and/or unpublished take advantage of competitions aimed at new writers. Later on you won't be eligible.

28. Be careful when the rules call for unpublished authors. The definition can vary from anyone who isn't contracted to a major publishing house, to those who've never had so much as a letter to the editor in print.

29. Rules on published work vary too. Having work posted on your own blog, or an open writing forum, is considered published by many.

30. Pay particular attention on where, and where not, to put your name and contact information. I've been caught out myself by accidentally leaving information in the document's footer.

    RJK: You may also need to consider the metadata if submitting electronically. That is electronic information which says who generated the file amongst other things and is held within the file properties of the document.

31. PC: Do make sure you've given correct contact information where it is required. If organisers can't contact you, they can't award the prize.

32. Be sure you've sent the right entry fee in the correct way. If you haven't, your work won't be considered.

33. For anonymously judged competitions, avoid leaving clues on the entry, social media, forums etc. If the work cannot be judged fairly, it may be disqualified.

34. If the rules call for unpublished work, don't send something that's out elsewhere and then have to withdraw it if it's accepted. Although some competitions do allow this, it's a hassle for all concerned and there's the risk you'll forget and accidentally break the rules.

35. Check the small print. I can't overstress the importance of understanding ALL rules. Will the organisers claim copyright? Can they use the work even if you don't win? Are you inviting persuasive pitches from vanity publishers? Will you have to attend an event to claim the prize or take part in publicity? These things don't mean you definitely shouldn't enter; just think carefully beforehand.

Check the small print

36. If you're not eligible, or chose not to enter for any reason, you can still use competition themes or prompts as inspiration.

37. If there's a maximum number of words it's probably wise to get close to that. A 1,000 word story is unlikely to have the depth and complexity of a 5,000 word one.

38. Actually enter the competitions! Reading winning entries feeling sure you could have done better won't get you anywhere.

39. Simply having completed something and sent it in can be a big boost to your confidence and you're already ahead of everyone who didn't try.

Don't miss deadlines

40. Don't miss deadlines. Postal delays, email problems and time zone differences should be allowed for.

41. Try competitions with entry restrictions, if you're eligible, as there'll be less competition. I've seen them limited by age, geographic location, gender, ethnic group, profession, or sexual orientation.

42. Those with very specific themes or complicated entry procedures have fewer entries. don't be put off by these and miss out on a good opportunity by attempting only the easier sounding ones. That's what everyone else will do.

43. Try micro or flash fiction competitions. There are lots which

ask for just 50 or 100 words. These make good creative breaks from longer projects.

44. Look out for fun competitions with tiny prizes, or which just offer glory. These tend to be less hotly contested. They're good practice, get you thinking, boost confidence if you win, yet won't result in huge disappointment if you don't.

45. Don't rule out really prestigious competitions with huge prizes. Of course there will be loads of entries and yours will need to be incredible to stand out – so write something incredible!

46. Typos in the title or opening paragraph severely damage your chances, as judges will be reluctant to trust you enough to engage with your characters and plot.

47. Ideally don't make errors anywhere. Proofread carefully, more than once. If a judge is struggling to choose between stories typing 'there' for 'their' could make the difference.

Submit only your own work

48. Submit only your own work. I know that seems obvious, but people do enter stuff they've 'found' and finished, rewritten or edited.

49. Don't fall foul of copyright by using characters or worlds created by someone else or include song lyrics you've not written yourself. If the organisers can't publish your work they'll not want to award it a prize.

50. If there's a theme, keep in mind that your first idea may have occurred to other entrants.

51. Don't abandon a great idea just because it came to you straight away. If it appeals strongly then maybe it's the story you should write.

52. Can you put a twist on the theme? Perhaps set it in the past or future, or write from an unexpected POV. Wedding stories don't demand brides as central characters – try the organist or cake baker, but do make the plot important to them.

53. Some themes occur repeatedly. Seasons, festivals, love, loss, change. You could prepare first drafts of likely ones in

advance and edit to suit the competition.

54. If you're asked to set the work in a Greek village, find out about local customs, food and places of interest. Don't write something based on your trip to Tenerife, or which could be set anywhere.

55. Start the piece with the first word of the action. If yours begins with a page describing the main character waking up, followed by two about the weather, the reader might be tempted to skim through the rest and so miss the good bits.

> Start with the action

56. Select the best word to express the meaning whilst matching the tone of the rest. Be sure it's used, and spelled, correctly.

57. If you can, get feedback on your entry from a trusted friend. As well as checking for readability and errors, ask how well it fits the theme.

58. Write something good and enjoy writing it. These things don't become less important just because it's a competition.

59. Ideally write something new for each themed competition. Adding a few words, or quickly making changes to shoehorn stories into the required category is unlikely to be successful. (But if you do happen to have something which actually fits, give it a polish and send it in.)

60. If emailing, double check you've attached the document and it's in the requested format. If judges can't read it, you can't win.

61. Take the entry to the post office and get it weighed. The organisers might not bother to trek down the sorting office and pay the excess charge if you guess wrongly.

62. Unless specified, double space, indent paragraphs, use a boringly easy to read font at a decent size. Judge's with headaches from squinting will feel less generous.

63. White paper. Black ink.

> Meet the brief

64. Meet the brief. If it's a story competition don't send poetry, or a novel extract.

65. Where possible read previous winning entries. If every single

one is a serious narrative, you might want to rethink that saucy limerick.

66. If you know who the judges are, research them. They're likely to have mentioned the competition on a blog, social media or their column as appropriate. If they've tweeted 'I hope there are/aren't lots of gnomes,' take heed.

67. Read the judge's work if you can. They won't expect, or want, you to write just as they do, but reading them can help you get on their wavelength.

68. Try to make your title interesting and unusual. You don't want your entry to get confused with a less good one of the same name. A brilliant title could be the deciding factor if two entries are very close.

69. Don't use unpronounceable words in the title. They won't stick so easily in the judge's mind.

70. Avoid offensive or swear words in the title. Judges may feel uncomfortable referring to your piece and therefore not plead its case to others on the judging panel. Organisers may be reluctant to mention it in the longlist.

71. Remember 'first-readers' and judges are human and will be actively looking for excuses to rule out stories to make the process more manageable. Don't help with that. Make sure you're well within the word count (however they count hyphenated words). If the competition requires you to write to a theme or prompt, be sure it's clear that you've done this.

72. Many competition entries are serious, even grim. Try humour as a change, the judge may appreciate it.

73. Make your entry memorable for the right reasons; distinct characters, vivid scenes, strong endings.

74. Competition entries don't usually have to comply with the tight guidelines produced by many publications, so can be a good place to experiment with different approaches or tackle subjects you wouldn't usually consider. Or perhaps the theme, or prize, will entice you into trying a form you rarely attempt.

75. Tell friends you'll enter so you can't back out. Make entering competitions a group activity and offer each other support.

76. Don't rush your entry. If there's time, put it aside between drafts and before the final read through, to help you spot weak areas and typos.

77. Give it a go. Even if you don't get the entry finished on time or it won't fit the word count, you'll have made a start on something which you might finish and sell elsewhere.

78. Keep records of which pieces of writing have been entered in which competition.

> Keep records of which story you send where

79. Check places such as *Writing Magazine*'s competition special and make an entry schedule so you can plan your writing, and don't accidentally send out work you'd earmarked for a particular competition.

80. Even if it's free entry and just a bit of fun, send something you're pleased with.

81. Writing to deadlines motivates you to actually finish something.

82. Don't simply wait for the results. Enter more competitions to increase your chances of success.

83. Keep a copy of your work.

84. Some competitions may raise money for, or awareness of, a particular cause so there will be winners other than those who're placed by the judges.

85. Paid markets for work are limited, especially for poetry. Competitions are another possible outlet as well as income generator.

86. Cross fingers, pick four-leaved clovers, kiss leprechauns. Luck does help.

87. Have a good internet presence. Some competitions are decided by public vote. The more online friends you have, the bigger pool of potential voters.

88. Check results. Sometimes you'll have to claim the prize, or you might be invited to a ceremony. Mistakes can happen meaning you're not informed in good time.

> Check results

89. Chase up prizes which are due to you if necessary. You earned it.

90. Judging, being a first-reader, or the person checking eligibility can give you a good insight into how competitions work.
91. Pay attention when winners announce their good luck. Many competitions are annual, or monthly, so you can try to emulate their success
92. Try not to take results too personally. If there are several well written entries, deciding on the winner will always be subjective to some extent.
93. Not winning isn't the same as losing. You were probably just one place behind those who got a mention anyway.
94. You're not limited to just one attempt. There are thousands of competitions to try, so you need never give up.
95. Don't let a win cause trouble with the tax man. Usually prizes are exempt, but if you write for a living, and/or claim entry fees against tax they might not be. Ask if you're not sure. (See the section on tax for more details.)
96. Running a writing competition can bring lots of benefits. Encourage your writing group to hold one, or have one on your blog.
97. Win or lose, your entries will be read – that's why you write!
98. Keep trophies polished so they aren't overlooked. They're great conversation starters and really annoy the mother-in-law.
99. Be gracious in victory or defeat. Gloating or sour grapes are strictly for losers.

Keep bubbly on ice!

100. Everyone gets a consolation prize of a piece to submit elsewhere. My first ever publication was a failed competition entry.
101. Keep bubbly on ice, chocolate in the cupboard or luxury bath oil on standby. If you follow all these tips you'll soon have something to celebrate and enjoying your win is the most important part of entering writing competitions.

EXERCISE 1

Research upcoming competitions and write an entry for at least one of them.

EXERCISE 2

Read the winning entries from a recent competition. Can you see why they won? Compare your own entry, if you made one, to see how you might improve it for next time you send it out.

OTHER MARKETS

RJK: We've already looked at the women's magazine market, but not every story is suitable for those and not every writer wants to write commercial fiction. Now let's look at the other options for your work.

Whichever market you decide to pursue, it is equally true that you need to get to know that market before submitting. Read stories that have been accepted. Look at things such as title length, story length, restrictions on subject matter as well as style and genre. The more research you do before submitting your work the more effective your submissions are likely to be. Submitting should never be a scatter gun approach with work sent out randomly, in the hope that one or other editor will like it. This will not endear you to editors and will mean you face a much higher than necessary number of rejections. By this stage it should also go without saying that your starting point should be to read and follow to the letter any submission requirements.

> Target submissions carefully

One thing to bear in mind is that stories which win competitions are very rarely ones you would be able to sell to women's magazines. A competition entry will normally need to be more complex, or challenge the reader further, than stories intended as a quick, light coffee break read. There are some that could successfully sit in either place, but those are few and far between.

In addition to the areas already covered earlier in the book, the main writing magazines carry competitions for short stories in every issue. *Writers' Forum* and *Writing Magazine* are the most widely read, but it is also worth looking at *Mslexia*, although this is only for women writers. As with any market, when choosing to submit stories to one of the writing magazine competitions, do read previous winners before submitting, as you will find the styles of successful stories quite different and that may directly influence which you choose to submit to. *Writing Magazine* provide a very good listing of competitions for fiction.

Genre writing

What if you write in another genre than commercial fiction? You will find many and varied outlets for every genre. Some of those will be paid and some cannot afford to offer any payment. Choose carefully according to what you are looking to achieve with your work. You may be happy for your stories to appear for free if you want to gain a publishing history for your cv, or to increase the exposure of your writing. However, if you want to earn money from your writing choose only those markets that will offer some form of payment.

> There are many and varied outlets for every genre

www.christopherfielden.com offers listings of magazines and other markets for short stories by country. It is not a complete list but is a useful place to look. The other big database is Duotrope www.duotrope.com They offer a free trial but then the information is accessed on subscription. It is a very thorough tool, listing hundreds, if not thousands, of outlets for your work.

Let's look at one sample market:

If you write mystery stories you may think it is a limited market, but a little research will reveal a large number of outlets including many paid ones. For example:

Alfred Hitchcock Mystery Magazine
The Strand
Mysterical E
Mystery Time
Futures
Sherlock Holmes Mystery Magazine
Ellery Queen Mystery Magazine

You'll find just as many outlets for crime stories, erotica, horror, fantasy or any other genre you care to write.

Radio

There are opportunities for short fiction in both local and national radio, but they can be hard to find. BBC Writers Room is a good starting point. Hospital radio may be another option if you want to hear your work broadcast to a more limited audience.

Newspapers

Some newspapers will carry a short story occasionally. National papers are unlikely to carry unsolicited material, but a local paper might, especially if your story has a particularly relevant angle to it. It is unlikely that you will be paid for this.

PC: There are also glossy 'county' magazines with titles such as *Hampshire Now* and *Yorkshire Life* which may accept fiction. Again stories with a local slant are most likely to be successful.

Small and specialist publishers

RJK: There are a number of publishers who produce magazines, online magazines, anthologies and single author collections. Some that are well known for specialising in short stories are Bridge House Publishing, Salt Publishing and of course Alfie Dog Fiction. A good source of information of other publishers putting together short story collections can be found at www.thejohnfox.com/publishers-of-short-story-collections/

Good source of information:

Web based

Web based publishers often accept previously published work, so can be used as a second (or third) bite of the cherry. The main ones are:

Amazon singles – 5,000 to 30,000 words – It gives a way of

highlighting the work though the Amazon platform. Ebook only. Usually you bring it out on the Amazon Kindle Direct Publishing (KDP) platform first.

Alfie Dog Fiction – Adult fiction 1,000 to 10,000 words, children's fiction from 500 words. Multiple download formats with authors earning royalties when their story is downloaded. Also produce collections which are available in paperback. Unlike Amazon, all stories are reviewed and those accepted are edited before publication.

Ether Books – Downloaded using a special application for android and Apple products. Many are given for free, there is a charge for submitting more than four stories.

Penny Shorts – Stories given for free with donations asked for, which go into an 'author pot'.

Everyday Fiction – Flash fiction download site (up to 1000 words) which does pay $3 for each item it uses.

The Fiction Desk – Open submissions and competitions with cash payment, however a £3 submission fee is charged per story.

Flash Fiction Online – For fiction from 500 to 1000 words with payment at $0.02 per word.

There are also hundreds of unpaid markets. You have to decide whether they will give your work the right profile to make them worth using. Do not be drawn into the belief that if you give enough of your work for free you will develop a fan base who will then buy your work – it can happen, but the more usual take up is people who look for free stories and then... more free stories.

PC: If you decide to submit somewhere which doesn't pay, be sure they don't simply publish everything they're sent. There's no merit in that and having work published which is either of poor quality itself, or seen alongside other substandard pieces could harm your future writing career.

Also remember you're still giving up 'first rights' and so can't offer these elsewhere.

Sources of information

RJK: In addition to the websites listed above it can be worth looking at *The Writers' and Artists' Yearbook*. Whilst this is not primarily directed towards short stories it is still worth looking at with over 4000 listings and there are publishers who will consider short story collections. *The Novel and Short Story Writer's Market* is a USA publication, but worth looking at and more tailored to short story writers.

EXERCISE

Make a list of the suitable markets for the genre you like to write in. Choose one as a target and write a story to send to it.

SOCIAL MEDIA AND THE INTERNET

PC: Social media can be very useful to writers in lots of ways – it's great for chatting to other authors, connecting with readers, story research, getting information on competitions and markets. Most agents and publishers will expect you to have some kind of internet presence, as will readers interested in finding out more about you and your work.

It can also help with marketing our work to some extent, but do remember the social part. If all you do is try to sell your books, you'll be as popular as... well, as somebody who does nothing but try to sell their books all the time. Usually doing this will simply result in being ignored, but on some sites and in groups it can get you banned.

Blogging

RJK: In the internet age blogging has become an important part of the social media presence. Many writers blog. It is a quick way to engage with your readers and can be used in different ways.

> Blogging is a quick way to engage with your readers

When I began to write full-time I started a blog that was the world through the eyes of our new puppy. We were living abroad and I thought it was a good way for the family to keep up with what we were doing. My plan was to write every day for around twelve months. That was over ten years ago. In that time 'Alfie' has missed one day of his blog, due to unforeseen circumstances. The blog has won awards, developed a global readership and been used to teach English as a foreign language. It has led to three books 'co-authored' with my dog. Now due to his advancing years Alfie has delegated some days to Aristotle and some to

Wilma so that he gets more chance to put his paws up.

On my own writing website I accidentally started a blog about me and my writing, but every so often find myself writing articles on writing advice or whatever is on my mind.

Blogging can be great fun and can be a way to build an audience for your writing. It can be a showcase for your work, but a word of caution, if you publish your work on a blog then when submitting it elsewhere you cannot claim it has not been published. The point of places wanting work that has not been published is usually because they are trying to earn a living and pay writers. If your work is freely available somewhere else, why would anyone want to pay to read it? If you want to submit a story to a magazine or other publisher, then do not publish it yourself on an open internet page.

> Blogs can take
> up a lot of time

PC: Another word of caution; blogs can take up a lot of time. As well as writing them, you may well wish to reply to comments and visit the blogs of your regular commenters. There's no law which says you must do these things, but you'll develop more of a relationship with your readers, and get more visitors, if you do. You can use blogs to interact with other writers even without having one of your own, by regularly commenting on those you find interesting.

There are a number of different blogging platforms, many of them free. Blogger and Wordpress are the best known and both are simple to use once you get used to them. With some you have the option of 'hosting' adverts and thereby earning money, but you need a huge audience for this to be worthwhile.

On our own blogs we can do anything we like, including constant sales pitches for our books. However, we're far more likely to get readers if we offer more than this. More readers for our blogs means more people will see the mentions of our books when we do post them. Perhaps we'll provide information, or some kind of service, but that isn't essential. Humour, sharing your experiences or pictures of cute animals can also be popular.

I have two writing blogs:

www.patsy-collins.blogspot.com 'Words about writing and writing about words'. This is a blog about my own writing life and love of words. There's a regular 'Wednesday word of the week' plus frequent links to free to enter writing competitions.

www.womagwriter.blogspot.co.uk This has news about fiction in women's magazines, interviews with writers and others associated with the industry and links to current guidelines.

Twitter

Twitter is probably the least time consuming form of social media. Each tweet is a maximum of 140 characters including spaces. You can add links and pictures, but these reduce the number of characters available for your message. You can tweet a thought or observation, share a joke or ask a question. Responses, if any, are usually very quick. Twitter moves fast and it's easy to miss things, especially if you follow a lot of people.

You need to follow people to see their tweets in your timeline and no one sees yours until they follow you. Start by following anyone whose tweets seem as though they may be interesting. You can easily unfollow again.

The easiest way to interact with others and make friends is to 'retweet' someone else's message. Just click the appropriate button and the message will appear in your timeline, thereby increasing the potential readership. You can also reply to comments, or click the heart to show you like something. Often if you regularly interact with people they'll follow you back, but they're not obliged to do so.

Hashtags help you find tweets and tweeters of interest. Some to search for are #writing #amwriting or # followed by the genre or issue you're looking for. You can add hashtags to your tweets too. (Note no spaces are used in these.)

#writingchat is a regular Twitter event I set up with a couple of friends. To take part just tweet on Wednesday evenings from 8-9 (UK time) using the hashtag.

> Join #writingchat on Wednesday evenings

Twitter is free to use.

My Twitter name is @PatsyCollins. Rosemary is @therealalfiedog

Facebook

RJK: A Facebook presence is well worthwhile for a writer, even if you also have a web page. It is a more immediate medium and gives you the ability to reach a wider audience and appear on the news feeds of people who might only infrequently visit your website.

There are two ways of doing this and you will need to decide what works for you. I do both, which probably shows some indecision.

Firstly, you can use your standard personal profile to promote your work. Doing this will mean that you need to accept friend requests from a wider range of people than you would do otherwise. You either need to be very careful about the personal material you then post, or select the group of people who will see a post without inadvertently broadcasting your family life to a wider audience. It can be done, but you will need to think very carefully about privacy. The other downside, is that your everyday friends may not want to be bombarded with constant reminders of your latest books or story successes.

PC: In theory you can keep things private on the internet, but to be safe, never post anything you're not happy to have become public knowledge.

RJK: Secondly, I have heard it advocated that you maintain two personal profiles, one for yourself and one for your writing. DO NOT do that. It is against the rules of Facebook and you risk being banned from the site altogether. Facebook has set up a clear method of working if you have a public profile and it can work very well. What they expect you to do, is to create a Facebook page. It can act in some ways like your website, but sits within Facebook. Many people use it instead of having a website.

A Facebook page is worthwhile for every writer

You set your Facebook page up by selecting the button for 'Create Page'. It will then take you through a series of options including making it clear what type of page you are creating. Once it's done you can promote your writing, organise online book launch events, start discussions on your writing, show your book covers or whatever you think will support your writing. You can invite people to 'like' your page to get followers and ask friends to share the link more widely. You can also include a link both to and from your website and include the address of the page on your business cards or at the back of the books you publish. Do make sure you take the option to change the page name from the allocated number to your name to personalise it. My page is www.facebook.com/rjkind/ and the one for Patsy is www.facebook.com/PatsyCollins.writer

Pinterest

I am the first to admit that I am not the world's most accomplished social media expert. However, having come to Pinterest relatively late, I have discovered things it can be very useful for.

In format, Pinterest is the electronic equivalent of your cork board on the wall. Whereas at home you might pin recipes torn from magazines, notes about when the cat's medication is due and the phone number of the local doctor, on Pinterest you can do all the online equivalents. Whatever you come across on the internet that you want to save and come back to, you can pin to a board on Pinterest. If you have a particular interest in dolphins, you might pin all the great dolphin pictures you find to a board. Others may then follow your dolphin board and go and look at the same sites.

There are two ways this can be useful as a writer. The one I have found most useful is to pin research material for a book I'm working on, or ideas I come across that I want to use in my writing at some point. It goes beyond noting the website address on which you found the material and lets you pin a specific image, while retaining the information of where it can be found. One example for me is a map of the street layout of New York in 1850, so I could check back to make sure I get the road names right and the walking direction of my characters correct.

The other way some writers use it is to promote their own work. Here I haven't got much further than pinning my own book covers so they can be seen, but you can use it for images linked to stories you publish or possibly better still to develop a board for the fans of your novel, with some of the key settings and landmarks in your work. To be quite honest, the possibilities are as limited as the imagination you apply to it. As I look around other boards I start to see wider potential waiting to be exploited.

Youtube

PC: This is a site which allows you to upload your own films. They're usually short. Quality is very variable! It's great for finding out how to do all sorts of things, so a brilliant research tool. If you want to describe your character tying a cravat, filleting a fish or shearing sheep, you can log on and watch someone do it.

If you have a camera which records films, you might like to consider producing a 'how to' piece on a topic related to your book, do an online reading or talk, or create a book trailer.

Personal websites

RJK: Most writers reach a point where they conclude that having a personal website is essential. It is your portal to the world. The best way you can present yourself and your writing to a wider audience. Not everyone feels they have the skills to set up a page, but with modern day packages such as Wordpress it can be very straightforward and relatively low cost. You can use a page on a free site, but the downside of this is that if for any reason you want to change which software you use, or they cease trading then you will have to change your website address and may lose some of your following. Ideally, buy your own domain name. Make sure your website's name both promotes your writing and is easy to write down correctly. The simpler it is the better. Mine is simply www.rjkind.co.uk Patsy's is www.patsycollins.uk.

What you put on your website is up to you, but this is you advertising yourself and your work. The style may vary according to whether you are writing for adults or children. If writing for adults you might have a dark and slightly sinister background if

> Writers often conclude a personal website is essential

you write horror, but would not want that if you focus on romance. Think carefully about how easy the pages are to read, as well as the words you use. Fancy fonts and highly coloured background do not make for easy reading. Look at a wide range of other sites before settling on what you are going to do. Even do sketches of what you want the final pages to look like before you make a start in setting them up. If you don't know how to do it yourself and your teenage child does, then offer them a small amount of pocket money if they will do it for you, as it will probably be cost effective. However, one word of caution if you do that, don't leave the design to them. Make sure you give them a proper brief of what it should look like and proofread it before it goes live.

Make sure readers who come to your site know where they can buy your work and check regularly to make sure the links are still valid. If a reader follows a broken link they only occasionally tell you and even less often do they scour the internet to find what it should have been.

There are tools you can use which show your progress on a current writing project, others which enable you to incorporate a blog of direct book sales. If you don't want to sell your book yourself, and they are available on Amazon, then get yourself set up as an 'Amazon Associate' so you can also earn commission on sales through that channel. Similar schemes are available with other sellers.

> **Keep your website up to date**

Check your website regularly for information that needs to be updated. If you say you have published two short stories when you are now up to fifteen you will be underselling yourself. It does mean regular checks and maintenance, but it is important.

PC: Give people a reason to keep coming back. This could be a regularly updated blog, news or pictures page. Some authors provide 'free samples' in the form of complete short stories or excerpts from a novel. You might mention special offers, or give links to free downloads. Perhaps you could run a competition?

It's a good idea to include a way for readers to contact you. This could be as simple as giving your email address, although contact forms seem the most usual option.

Forums/Online writing groups

RJK: Patsy and I originally met through *Writing Magazine*'s Talkback Forum. It is a community of writers where you can share ideas, ask questions, have a laugh and support each other in the lonely pursuit of writing. There are other such forums and it is well worthwhile having a look around to find one that suits you. Some are more about critiquing work, some are more about the social side of writing.

Alfie Dog Fiction and the whole idea of setting up a short story download site came out of friendships formed through Talkback. A few of us also set up our own critiquing group and help with each other's novels and short stories. I've also built relationships with cover designers and proofreaders through the same source.

Online writing groups have their place too. Not everyone can get to a physical writers' group easily. It may be that you live in the middle of nowhere, aren't available at specific meeting times or for some other reason simply cannot attend. There are some very good online groups which can help to fill the gap. Writers' groups can take many forms. I belong to ones which critique each other's work, develop ideas and work on writing projects and another which works on the basis of setting a number of writing challenges every three weeks for a period of the year and we all judge each other's work, anonymously. At the end of the season one of the group wins the virtual trophy and then we have a short summer break before it all starts again.

All of these are opportunities both to find support for your writing life and to receive input from likeminded people, who will help you to develop your writing.

EXERCISE

Go online now and make contact with at least one other writer. PC: But we're only allowing you ten minutes for this – it isn't a procrastination exercise!

NANOWRIMO

What it is

National Novel Writing Month (often just called NaNo) is the fairly mad idea of writing a 50,000 word novel during November. That's 1667 words a day. The nation concerned was initially the USA but it's now a worldwide event with tens of thousands of participants. There's a website you can sign up to, discussion forums to join, a 'winner' badge to download and merchandise to buy, but that's all optional.

Of course no normal person can write a decent novel in just one month. NaNo is really a method of quickly creating a first draft. Writing an entire novel draft in thirty days is a real achievement.

Should I give it a try?

That depends. If you're happy with the speed at which you produce first drafts then you don't need it. There's even a danger it could introduce bad habits into your writing, because of the emphasis on speed rather than quality.

On the other hand, if during the first draft stage, you find yourself spending hours forming one perfect sentence or constantly fiddling about with what you've already written and therefore making very little progress, it might be helpful. (Such attention to detail isn't always bad, but it discourages necessary rewrites. Most writers need to get the story written first and edit later.)

Generally, getting lots of words onto page or screen in a short period is a good thing. It's encouraging to see progress and it provides plenty of material to shape into the finished piece. A speedily written draft will almost certainly require a lot of work to make it good enough for publication, but it's a huge improvement on a blank page. Whether it's an improvement on two beautifully written paragraphs, only you can decide. Don't forget that drafts written slowly are also likely to need a great deal of work before they're ready for publication.

How could it help?

NaNo encourages you to turn off your 'inner editor' (the part of you which isn't satisfied with a sentence until it's as good as you can possibly make it). All too often we're more aware of the flaws in our writing than the strengths, and this can hinder progress. The speed at which you'll need to write, in order to finish your draft, leaves no time for doubts or procrastination.

Very few people will be able, or want, to write at such a frantic pace on a regular basis, but making the attempt

> 50,000 words
> in one month

even just once could leave you with a permanent improvement in your rate of progress. I've taken part several times and believe it's helped me in that way.

Variations

If you know 1667 words a day simply isn't possible for you, work out a realistic yet challenging target and work towards that. If it's a good result for you then it's a good result. If 50,000 doesn't seem much of a challenge, write 100k.

Although clearly designed for novelists, many short story writers also take part. You could either try to match the word count in separate pieces, or create thirty story drafts, regardless of length.

Tips for becoming a NaNo 'winner'

If you're not sure you'll need a scene, write it anyway. You can always delete it if it's not required.

If you get stuck on a scene make a note about what needs to be done and go on. Come back to researching minor points afterwards. If you realise you've made a mistake somewhere, make a note and come back later. Worried you're repeating yourself? Write anyway and keep the best version. Don't stop to read back what you wrote yesterday.

No more coffee until you've done 1,000 words. No bathroom breaks until you've done another 1,000. RJK: That will really make you find out just how fast you can write/type!

PC: Don't fret over punctuation. You'll probably change it later anyway and deciding between a comma and a semi colon takes as long as writing the words which will complete the sentence.

Unplug the phone. Disconnect the internet and email. Don't assume you can catch up at the weekend, or tomorrow after a better night's sleep. Do today's word count today. RJK: Get ahead if you plan to take any time out.

PC: Don't think too long about the story – just write it.

As you can see, it's all about moving the story forward and sorting everything out later. My advice, for anyone who would like to write more words in a limited time, is to attempt NaNo once. Even if you decide not to do it again, you'll have a better idea of how you like to work and a rough draft to edit.

EXERCISE

When you're ready, maybe not this year, sign up and have a go at NaNo. Good luck!

BLURB OR SYNOPSIS?

RJK: Many writers find the difference between a blurb and a synopsis difficult to understand. They serve completely different purposes.

A synopsis is the outline of the story INCLUDING how everything turns out.

A blurb is a hook to get the reader to want to read the story and NEVER gives away the ending.

Synopsis

Usually a synopsis will be asked for when sending a novel (or the opening chapters of a novel) to be considered for publication. It may be asked for with a short story, ensure you read submission guidelines.

> Synopsis – major detail of the plot, including ending

It covers the major detail of the plot – up to and including the way the story concludes. Given it should ideally run to only a single side of A4 with a normal type size and layout, it is not possible for it to mention every character or every twist and turn of the story.

However, in condensing it to this length it should still give a flavour of your writing style and be interesting. A two-dimensional, boring synopsis is not going to make a reader want to read your book and consider it for publication any more than a long-winded, meandering synopsis is. It needs to be punchy, interesting and sell your writing as well as the story.

The first time you mention a character's name it should be set in capitals. Subsequently, revert to typing the name as you normally would.

When writing a synopsis many writers are loathe to give away the ending, however it is essential. A publisher wants to know if the plot is realistic and plausible. They also want to know if it is too well worn and has been covered too much already. This is not the time to end it with something like 'and you'll have to read the book to find out what happens'.

Blurb

A blurb is the short piece on the back of a book, or the equivalent for a short story. It is what most readers look at before deciding if they want to read further. It is the challenge of the story in a nutshell - the hook. If you get it right the reader is desperate to read the story to find out what happens to your protagonist. It is unlikely to make mention of many characters - it focusses on the problem your hero or heroine faces. Very often it asks a question and leaves the reader really wanting to know the answer. Of course, the answer is not something they will find just by reading the first page! It is the question at the heart of the story. The whole reason they will need to read the entire thing.

> Blurb - short piece to hook the reader

Both a blurb and a synopsis are normally written in the present tense. This does not depend on what tense the book or story is written in.

If submission guidelines call for a blurb or a synopsis make sure you give the one that is called for and don't hedge your bets by giving both, or give something different from the requirements thinking you know better. A publisher specifies what they want for a reason and not because they've not thought it through!

Elevator pitch

> Two or three sentences which sell your story

A modern requirement is what is known as 'an elevator pitch'. Imagine you are in an elevator (lift in the UK) and there is another person there. You may only be sharing that space with them for a floor or two, which, presuming it is not an express lift, gives you chance to say maybe two or three sentences to impress them into buying your book.

These are not easy to construct. They need to hook the reader in a matter of very few words. You can put them together by starting with your blurb and paring it down. This may work, but be careful you do not end up with a relatively flat sentence or two that says what you mean but does so without sparking interest.

Tweet

Having reduced your book to three sentences, now condense that into no more than 140 characters including spaces.

> Your story in 140 characters

Why would you want a tweet length hook? For two reasons: Firstly, if you are trying to promote your book you are likely to be using social media. Reducing your book into a promotional line you can tweet is the best way to get people to read it using that channel. Secondly, if you are looking for a publisher or agent for your work then some of them have occasions when they will accept a pitch by Twitter. If they like your tweet they ask to see more. You get one or at most two shots to impress them and need to use them effectively.

Just to make it even harder, they are likely to ask you to include the book title and a hash tag to ensure the tweet is picked up, thus reducing your character count.

Example

I'm not going to include the full synopsis but here by way of example are the Blurb, Elevator Pitch and Tweet for *The Appearance of Truth*.

Blurb:

When 30 year old Lisa Forster begins to trace her family tree, she discovers her birth certificate belonged to a baby who died at four months old and is not in fact her own. Her apparently happy middle class upbringing was a myth and her parents had a dark secret.

With Pete Laundon's help Lisa sets about searching for the truth. She follows up all possible routes, until with no options left she goes to the newspapers for help. After 30 years, who if anyone knows: Who is Lisa Forster? Why was she never told? And who was the baby who died?

The Appearance of Truth is the gripping tale of one woman's search for identity.

Elevator pitch:

Lisa Forster discovers the birth certificate she has had for thirty years belonged to a baby who died at the age of four months old and is not her own. Her apparently happy middle class upbringing is a myth and her parents had a dark secret. The story is the gripping search for who she really is.

Tweet:

Her birth certificate belongs to a baby who died, so who is Lisa Forster?

EXERCISE

Describe your current piece of writing in less than 100 words.

KEEPING TRACK OF SUBMISSIONS

Why you need to do this

PC: It is absolutely vital to keep good records of which story is sent where and what the response was. If you don't, you are at risk of breach of copyright, breaking competitions rules and missing opportunities. Many places don't permit simultaneous submission, or accept previously published work. Not knowing which story went where makes it impossible to avoid these things, unless you only ever submit freshly written pieces.

Good records also help you target your submissions to better effect. Knowing how long you must wait for replies helps when submitting seasonal work. Understanding which type or length of stories get the best results from a particular market enables you to improve your chances. If you earn any money from your writing, then accurate records will also be needed to avoid trouble with the tax man.

> Good records help you target your submissions

People forget things! I won't ever forget my first acceptance, but I can't tell you which was my seventh rejection, or list every story I've sent to a particular magazine, or remember if I ever got a reply to that one about the horse I sent in February. Or rather, I couldn't without referring to my records.

Types of records

How you keep records is up to you, but do devise a system which is simple to use and will continue to be so in the future. Index cards per story, or a sheet in a notebook, are fine for the first dozen stories, but less convenient when you've written a few thousand. If you're a novelist, they may well be perfect throughout your career. For poets or flash fiction writers they'll have cascaded to the floor, squishing the cat, before a year is out. The same goes for notebooks or any other paper system.

If you can already manage spreadsheets or a database, I strongly suggest using one. Using filters allows searches to be carried out with very little effort. Being able to look quickly at everywhere a story has been, or everything still awaiting a decision or all the work sent to one particular market or all stories in a particular word count range is jolly handy.

> Use standard terminology to make searching easier

RJK: Make sure you use standard terminology so that you can search easily. If you call a word count 1,000 word one time and 1,050 words the next, or decide to be precise and put 998 words, then it will make searching and filtering more difficult. Whilst this may sound obvious, it can become more tricky when trying to describe the subject matter of stories.

PC: They can be colour coded too, should you ever be short of a procrastination activity.

Other records you might wish to keep are dates for submission windows and competition deadlines, to do lists, check lists for different projects (especially if you're self-publishing), research resources used, people to include in acknowledgements and possibly you'll want to chart how much time you've spent writing, or the number of words written per day. These will depend on your projects and your personality, but all writers really must record submissions and income received. (We will come back to the accounting and tax side later.)

What I do

My short story submissions, starting with the first one ever in 2002, are recorded on a spreadsheet. The headings are:

- Story title. I suggest keeping the same title in all records and having a different column for name changes if there are any.
- Where submitted to

- Date of submission
- What type of submission it is – competition, unsolicited, commissioned etc.
- Date of acknowledgement (if any)
- Word count – to the nearest 100 words
- Response – rejection, shortlist, acceptance etc. – and date of that
- Date to chase up – based on normal response times or when competition results are due
- How submitted – post, email, online form, Payment due – and date this is received

You may want to add notes on how the story was submitted, reason for rejection, suggestions for where to send it next if returned, genre, pen name used or anything else you think might be useful.

I keep my financial records on spreadsheets too, but we have a whole section on this.

I'm sure Rosemary will back-up my claim that I'm not particularly technically minded, but I've mastered the basics of spreadsheets – and the basics are all you'll need. If you have a friend or family member who is better at this kind of thing, ask them to set it up for you and show you how to enter information and carry out simple searches.

Start now

If you think you might need to do this in the future, start now. Transferring in old data would be very boring and, if it includes lots of rejections, quite demoralising.

RJK: My system is very similar to Patsy's. I did start years ago with record cards, but it very soon became apparent that these had a limited life. A spreadsheet is definitely a good approach. However, don't rush into it. The time you take thinking exactly how you want to set your work up, will save you having to go through a whole lot of work later when it dawns on you you've missed columns you would find useful. Most importantly, make sure it is backed up!

Using records

PC: As already mentioned, they can help with targeting new submissions. Perhaps they'll show there are stories which you never got around to submitting, or have only been tried with one market. They may also reveal gaps in your story stock. Maybe you have no Christmas stories, or 700 worders left. They'll show if you've not tried a particular market for a while, or maybe that you already have lots out with one and are in danger of swamping them if you send more.

You may have to 'chase up' stories if you don't get a reply. Never just assume that because they've said no to the one you sent in July that the one sent in June can now be sent elsewhere. Don't chase before a reasonable period is up. I'd give it three months at least and longer if any guidelines advise this, or you happen to know they usually take longer. Your records may show if that's the case, or you may find out from other writers.

RJK: You will also need to check that payments have been received and remind the appropriate person if this seems to have been overlooked. Once work is published, your records act as a reminder to add the details to ALCS or PLR (see glossary for details) if appropriate – don't forget to note you've done this.

PC: Looking back on records can be quite motivating. If I scroll back to 2002 I can see I made very few submissions (mainly because I'd not written much) and had even fewer acceptances and wins. Oh, O.K. then; I had a single competition placing for a 50 word story. The next year I wrote and submitted three times as much and there are three entries in the accepted column. My output hasn't trebled each year, but it has gone up. So have the number of acceptances and the percentage of stories which are successful. Even if you don't yet have acceptances to record, you should be encouraged to see stories 'out there' and know that any one of those could result in that first publication.

To do lists

I think these are best done on paper, mainly because of the pleasure which is gained by crossing off completed items, but you

> Don't rely on remembering all the things you planned to do – Write them down

may prefer another system. One of my lists is of writing tasks, both general and specific. There are always some quick, simple or easy tasks as well as more challenging ones. E.g. 'update blog', 'buy stamps', 'research infectious diseases' or 'write short story'. I don't write every day, but it's very rare for me not to get something crossed off.

In addition, I have a sheet for each of the next twelve months. On these I write the title of every magazine I'd like to submit to and then as I have stories ready, either newly written or returned from elsewhere and edited as needed, I write in the titles. The blanks help me decide where to concentrate my efforts next. Details of competition closing dates go on there too.

RJK: I'm a list compulsive and use both the computer and handwritten. On the computer I have a to do list with dates ahead, so that I don't touch a piece of work again until it is due for completion. I also have a system that has reminders for recurring tasks so they come up only when they are due and I don't have to remember any of them. I then use paper to sort my day out in order, slotting in those tasks I don't want to do amongst the more fun ones. Then all I have to do is make myself do them! On the bright side, people often ask how on earth I remember things, and now you know!

Other admin matters

PC: Consider having a dedicated email for submissions. That means there's less risk of you missing anything important in among the spam and Facebook updates.

> Have a dedicated email for submissions

Whether it's a separate one or not, do ensure it's 'sensible' and professional (not sexy-totty69). Just your name is best.

RJK: You would be amazed how many people send serious work from frivolous email addresses. Your email says something about you, make sure it's the right something.

PC: It needs to be one you won't need to keep changing. The editor/publisher will try to contact you on the one you quoted on your submission, which may have been made months ago. If her offer to buy or request for a rewrite never reaches you, then the story probably won't get published.

RJK: If you change your email, it is your responsibility to let publishers know. Do not expect them to take the time to try to find you, or if they request electronic submissions, to go to the cost and trouble of trying to reach you by post. The onus is on YOU.

PC: If you move house, have mail forwarded – don't expect the editors to somehow know you no longer live where you did when you submitted.

Back everything up – ideally in several places.

Keep a supply of paper, envelopes and stamps. The former are cheaper bought in bulk and you don't want to miss a competition deadline because the post office is closed.

Don't overdo it

There is a lot of paper, and a lot of computer documents, involved in writing. You may save different drafts of your stories, gather vast amounts of research material, amass a heap of rejection slips, save useful articles and calls for submission, collect every magazine you're published in, create masses of lists and plots and mind maps.

You'll need all this stuff, at least for a while. A few things you'll want to keep forever, but most are soon clutter at best and could cause you serious problems. There's a risk of fire for one thing! More likely is that if you have old guidelines lying around you'll use them instead of the current ones, or multiple versions of a work in progress will cause you to work on, or submit, the wrong one. If you hang on to things you don't need, it becomes increasingly difficult to store and locate what is important.

Get rid of what you don't need – starting with rejection slips once you've recorded the details. I shred mine and put them on

Keep acceptances and throw out rejections

the compost heap and eventually they are used to grow me beautiful flowers. Isn't that better than having them block the route to my desk?

RJK: It's also much cheaper to throw them out than buy filing cabinets and reinforcing the floors. However, DO NOT throw out your financial records, you need to keep most of those for six years plus the current tax year!

PC: Financial records are kept on separate sheets of my submissions workbook. I start a new one each for income and expenditure each financial year. They have the same headings as used for tax returns, making it very simple to transfer the information across and submit my accounts online. This is covered in more detail on the section on finance.

EXERCISE

Set up a submissions file, if you don't already have one. If you do have one, ensure you are recording all the information you are going to need in the years of successful writing to come.

REASONS FOR REJECTION

There are many reasons why a story is rejected. Most new writers immediately assume the editor is saying their work is not good enough, self-doubt is never far from the shoulder of most of us. However, if

> A rejection does not mean your work is not good enough

the editor has only just accepted a very similar story, then however good yours is, it is likely to be rejected. Sometimes it is as simple as the editor is having a bad day and almost everything they read will be rejected. At other times they are so inundated with submissions that although with only a small amount of editing yours would be good enough, they simply don't have the time to devote to it.

PC: Some publications receive hundreds of submissions each month and can only use a small fraction of them, so may well have to reject stories which meet all their requirements.

RJK: It can be worth thinking about when you send your submissions. Most writers are not able to work on their writing full-time, but fit it around other jobs. Therefore, they are most likely to submit work at weekends, in evenings or at holiday times. Those are the times that editors are most likely to want to spend a little bit of time away from their desks. They will either only give a small amount of time to things they look at then, or arrive on Monday morning or post-holiday to find an inbox full of submissions. If you can possibly do it, without running into a problem with your day job, submit during regular office hours other than a Monday. That way your submission is more likely to be noticed.

PC: Don't worry too much about this with the large circulation magazines as they don't tend to look at submissions until weeks, or even months, after they're sent, but with smaller publishers it might make a difference.

Make sure you send seasonal stories in plenty of time. A Christmas story received in November is very unlikely to be used, as the December issue will already be in the shops. If you're sending anything time sensitive, then make this clear on the envelope, or in the email header and in any covering letter, to help it get seen in time.

RJK: Most importantly, if your work is rejected by one editor – don't give up. Repackage it making sure you have met the submission requirements of the next possibility and send it out again... and again... and again, until it finds a home. If you are not certain that the standard is good enough for publication, ask your critiquing group or pay for a professional critique of some of your work to see where you are going wrong.

Send the story out again

Once you've done that send the story out again!

SECTION 5

A WRITER'S LIFE

A PROPER WRITING ROUTINE

PC: Some people advise writers to create writing routines, to be organised and methodical in their approach. 'Have a dedicated working area, even if it's just a corner of a room,' they'll say. 'Work out the best time for you to write and arrange things so you're always at your desk then.' You may be advised to see one project through before starting another. They may even suggest the best order in which to approach writing tasks.

A routine suits some people. I'm not sure many of those people are writers, but if you like this kind of approach and are in a position to implement it then don't let me put you off. I'm sure it's very sensible and nothing which works for you is wrong. However, if you have family, animals, or anything else which makes planning your time difficult, or if by nature you prefer to take a more casual attitude, don't use that as an excuse not to write. Just because you can't do it regularly, doesn't mean you shouldn't do it frequently.

> Just because you can't write regularly, doesn't mean you shouldn't write frequently

How do you know mornings are your most creative period if you've never tried writing at night? If you must work in a particular room for the words to flow, will you never move home? Suppose Tuesday evenings are your writing time – will you refuse each and every invitation for that time and do nothing on an unexpectedly free Saturday morning? Are you prepared to miss out on opportunities because meeting the deadline would mean leaving one project unfinished as you work on another?

You might like to learn about the methods of other writers and adopt them yourself. That's fine – if it works. Please don't be fooled into thinking that just because something suits a successful well known author, or your prolific writing buddy, or Rosemary, or me, that it must be right for you. Experiment until you find a working method you're happy with and which you can incorporate into the rest of your life. And then be prepared to adapt it whenever your circumstances change.

ACCOUNTS AND TAXATION

It's a hobby, do I have to keep accounts?

RJK: The simple and sensible answer is yes. If you make any money at all from your writing you need to declare it to the taxman (see below), keeping records from the start is therefore a good discipline to develop. Besides, in the early days your costs are likely to be more than the income from your writing and, as long as you are prepared to do a tax return, that will give you some losses that you can offset against income later on, to reduce what tax you pay.

What records should I keep?

You need to keep a record of all the costs you incur which are directly relevant to your writing. Not just the amounts, but the receipts as well. The best way to do that is on a spreadsheet. Record the date, where you bought the item from, what it was and the amount paid. To reduce complications, it will help to keep your records in years, not the calendar year, but the tax year. The tax year runs from 6th April one year to 5th April the next. Odd as that is, there are historic reasons for it and no one has seen fit to change it. If you keep your receipts in a plastic wallet you can start a new one for each year. Alternatively use something like a ring binder.

When I say the costs directly relevant to your writing that means things like the paper you print your work out on to send to a publisher, stamps for sending them, business cards, reference books. You can even include the cost of this book in your expenses as it serves no other purpose than helping your writing.

PC: Writing workshops and classes, plus the travel to get to them can also be claimed back. Research trips can too – as long as it really is research for writing and there's a chance you'll sell the pieces and not just a nice day out you'll mention on your blog.

RJK: If you buy a computer and you use it to email your granny in Australia, then unless your granny is also your editor and you are emailing her about your work, you cannot say the computer is completely for your writing. You may, if you are doing a lot of writing and sending work out for payment, be able to claim that a percentage of your computer is writing related, maybe 50%, but don't try claiming for the games applications you added as paid downloads, they are most certainly not!

When you are writing as a hobby, it is unlikely you are going to have an office dedicated to your work and, if you said you had, it might be questioned. However, if you are working as a writer full-time and earning your main living that way, then you can charge some of the costs of a home office as business expenses, but by that stage it is worth looking at this in much more detail than this book can go into.

You also need to keep a record of all income you receive from your writing, both directly from magazines or book sales, or indirectly from ALCS or PLR etc. The same goes for fees from speaking engagements about your writing, it all needs to be noted down.

You should also keep clear information on who owes you money for work and if there are any payments you need to make to other people.

Will I have to pay tax?

If your income from your writing is more than your expenses and you are over the tax threshold when this figure is combined with any other income, then yes you will need to pay tax on the profit from your writing.

Who is my employer?

In simple terms, you are your own employer. You are self-employed and you need to fill in a different set of pages on a self-assessment tax return to cover that. You don't need to include a great deal of detail unless you are making a lot of money, but you do need to tell HMRC what you are making. If you are outside the

UK then you are likely to find that the rules are something similar, but it is wise to check.

Do I have to pay tax on competition winnings?

If you are treating entry fees and other costs of entering competitions as a business expense, then yes you do need to declare the winnings as well. If you don't include those then it's not so straightforward. If you only occasionally enter and win competitions then probably not, however if you are effectively making a business out of your regular competition wins then HMRC may look at things differently. They have been clamping down on hobby income over the past couple of years so it is better to try to get it right.

PC: If you contact them and ask about any queries they're very helpful.

I'm speaking to a writers' group, are my travelling costs an expense?

RJK: Yes they are. Whether you go by public transport or in your own vehicle you can include the expense. For your own vehicle there are 'mileage rates' which you are allowed to charge against your taxable income, so record the distance and check the latest rate for the current tax year. Remember the cost of parking too.

Do I need a separate bank account?

Not necessarily, but it can be useful. It's also a way of letting your writing income accumulate so you can do something special with it.

How long do I need to keep my records for?

Basically, the answer to that is seven years; the current year plus the preceding six tax years. However, there are some items for which it may be longer. If you are setting up to earn your income from your writing and buying long term or 'capital' items, specifically for your writing business, then you may need to keep them for a longer period.

Do I need an accountant?

If you are methodical and make sure you set things down as they happen, the paperwork you need to complete is relatively straightforward and you are likely to be able to do it yourself. However, what you cannot afford to do is not keep records and get yourself into a mess. Then you will probably need to pay someone at some point to sort out the mess. Once you have a system set up it is best to keep on top of it.

I've been asked for an invoice what do I do?

Anyone can produce an invoice using a word processing package or a spreadsheet. You can even produce a handwritten one, although that may look less professional, or buy an 'invoice book'.

There are some pieces of information that legally must appear on your invoice:

It must state that it is an invoice. It must have a unique number and show both your name, address and contact information and those of the company or person you are invoicing. You then need to include information on what you are charging for, the amount being charged and the date of the invoice. You will only need to worry about VAT if your turnover reaches the level required (currently £83,000), for most writers that is not likely to be an issue.

It is also sensible to put on your invoice details of where payment should be made to, such as your bank account and sort code and the date by which you expect payment to be made. For example, you might say that you expect payment within fourteen days of the invoice date.

PC: If you use a pen name it's a good idea to state who the payment should be made to as well, to avoid confusion.

I haven't been paid for a piece of work what do I do?

RJK: Start by sending a polite email reminder checking they have the payment on their system and ask when you can expect for it to be paid. If that does not yield a response, follow it up with a telephone call to their purchase ledger department to find out what is happening. You may need to send through proof of what is owed, copy invoice, evidence of publication etc. Usually you will find that the payment has simply been overlooked, or is awaiting authorisation.

Do I pay National Insurance?

If you are not employed, then it can be worth voluntarily registering to pay national insurance. However, there are minimum figures below which that is not necessary (currently £5,965 for Class 2 and £8,060 for Class 4). In the early days of your writing it is unlikely that you need to consider it, but if you do start to make some money then you will be told what you owe when you submit your tax return.

LEGAL QUESTIONS

Copyright

Both when you sell your own work and whenever you use the work of others you must think about copyright. Let's start with copyright on your own writing.

Proving copyright

In years gone by, you were advised to mail a copy of all your work back to yourself in special tamper proof envelopes. The date on the post mark acted as proof, if you ever needed it, that the work was written prior to that date. If you ever found it used elsewhere it would be legal evidence of your ownership. Times have changed. Now, computer generated work has metadata attached to it. It is an electronic record of what has happened to that file. This could prove useful evidence, but better still is for there to be a copy that you have emailed to yourself or posted electronically to a secure location, which will also provide an audit trail of date and ownership. The critique group we are part of has created its own discussion board and we post work to that. It creates an audit trail, and back-up copies of the system provide permanent records.

Which rights do I sell?

The rights you give up will vary widely according to where the work is placed. In the extreme you will give up all rights in exchange for a fixed payment. From that point you may not republish that piece of work in any form. Your only option, in order to reuse any of it, would be to write a new, and completely different piece, using the same information.

Traditionally, magazines bought First British Serial Rights

(FBSR) or the equivalent in other countries. That meant you sold only the right to publish it for the first time in print format in that country. Usually there would be an agreed time period before you published the work elsewhere. That was before the digital age took over and the opportunities for publication broadened. Now it is not uncommon for a publisher to request worldwide rights for a period and ongoing (but not exclusive) digital rights. If that is the case then after whatever agreed length of time, you would be able to publish the work anywhere that is willing to consider previously published work, but you cannot be certain it will not also be published in some form by the previous publisher. What a writer needs to consider is the extent of the payment they receive compared to the rights they give up. If the publisher has retained rights to publish again in other formats it is not unreasonable to ask whether you will receive further payment for those repeat publications, or a higher up-front fee to reflect it.

Remember rights can be broken down into a wide range of options now. You have the audio rights, the digital rights and potentially the film rights to consider in addition to the rights to the traditionally printed word.

If you self-publish you retain the rights to your work. The same is true if you go through some online publishers, such as Alfie Dog Fiction, for short story downloads.

Quoting from other work

You may wish to quote from other work. If it is out of copyright, which in the UK means more than 70 years after the death of the author, then it is not a problem. However, if it is still covered by copyright then there are important considerations. There is a term 'fair usage' which allows a limited amount of work to be quoted in some circumstances, such as for the purpose of review. Bear in mind reproducing it within another commercial work is not specifically listed as an exception to the copyright law and so any quoting in a fiction context is open to a copyright infringement claim. Quoting from songs and poetry which is covered by copyright are generally considered no go areas and the music industry, in particular, does follow this up quite actively. If you want to quote from work which is still within copyright then the only safe option is to obtain written permission from the copyright owner first.

You may also need to think about some less obvious areas. Whilst many think that quoting from the Bible must be all right as it is such an old book, if you choose a modern translation then the translation is likely to be under copyright. Don't be lulled into quoting the King James' version instead. Copyright of that and the Common Prayer Book rest with the Crown and they may not be used for commercial purposes without permission. Restrictions also exist on some other translations so check into this carefully if you are considering using them.

I found an image on the internet, can I use it?

The best rule of thumb is 'not without permission'. Photographers and artists earn their living through their creative work in the same way that writers do. If you don't want someone to steal your work you need to be mindful that you don't steal theirs. Yes, there are Creative Commons licences on some things, but you need to read the small print to make sure how you are using the work falls into permitted use. Even if you pay for a downloaded image, there may be restrictions on how it can be used, so you need to read the detail and be certain. The biggest pitfall is where images are available for free download. Many people take this to mean free for any use, but the usual restriction is for non-commercial and educational purposes only. Using it for your book cover or in a story you are planning to sell is commercial use and therefore falls outside of this. This is all true of writing you find on the internet too. Respect the copyright of the originator of all creative work as you would wish them to respect your work. If you want to use something obtain written permission first.

I've found my work on someone else's website what do I do?

This happens rather too often. If you find your copyright has been breached, then you can issue a 'takedown notice' under the Digital Millennium Copyright Act (DMCA) to have the webpage removed. This is a piece of American legislation, but its use and application has been taken as fairly universal. There is legislation in the UK such as the Digital Economy Act 2010, and across the EU, but the international nature of the internet means very often it is the USA act which is referred to. The chances are the site you are calling on to take down the work will not be based in the UK anyway. The process is not complicated and does not need a lawyer. You can find information on how to do it on the internet. The notice is sent to the webhosting company for the offending site, so you don't have to deal with the individual who has committed the breach. It is a standard procedure and, as long as you have provided full information, the action should be executed by the webhosting company in a reasonable time. It is all too common and from personal experience, whilst following the process is a hassle we could well do without, it does work.

Libel

What happens if I write about real people?

If you are writing about real people, even those who died some years ago, it is important to publish only correct factual information. If you are creating a fictional story and for example make a famous person a thief in the story, then you are at serious risk of being sued for damages for libel. The cost of defending an action of that nature will not only be the end of your writing career, but of your house as well. It is not worth doing.

PC: Think carefully even if what you intend to write is the truth. Legal action isn't the only possible result of writing about real people. You may cause distress, friction within families, or end friendships.

What about using real products in my work?

RJK: Again this is a difficult area. If you are simply saying the character sipped a glass of Gordon's gin and tonic, then it could be seen as good advertising for the company and you are showing it in a good light as the drink of choice. If you take a product or company and make a negative comment or comparison, then unless you can substantiate what you have said then you are at risk once again. Bear in mind, even if you can prove what you are saying you will still have to face the cost of defending any action and a company's resources to take legal action are generally much greater than an individual's to defend one.

Contracts

When you have work accepted by a publisher it is normal to be asked to sign a contract. This is there to protect you as well as the publisher. You should read all of the details of the contract carefully and make sure you have understood what it says. Also, be sure to check it covers the things that are important to you, giving clarity on what rights you are giving up and what payment you will receive, and when!

Don't be afraid to ask for items in the contract to be clarified if they do not appear to cover what you are expecting. For your part, you are likely to be confirming that the piece is your own work and that if there is any possibility of the work belonging to someone else that will be your legal responsibility and not the publisher's. Of course, as long as you have not taken someone else's work, that will not be a problem.

WORKSHOPS AND CONFERENCES

PC: Writing workshops are a varied bunch. They can be offered as part of a larger event, such as a festival, run as a series, or be one offs. They may be quite general in approach, e.g. 'short story writing' or deal with one specific aspect of writing, such as dialogue. Running time can be anywhere from two hours to an entire week.

Costs can vary hugely too – from free to hundreds of pounds. Look carefully at what's being offered and how well it suits your current needs. If one of the justifications of a high price is the chance to meet agents or publishers, it might be best to wait until you have a book or two in which they may be interested.

Woman's Weekly offer an extensive package of writing workshops at £65 or £79 a day, plus the cost of getting to London or Manchester. They can be worthwhile if you wish to write for this market. One sale would more than cover your investment. *The People's Friend* also now offer workshops for people who'd like to write for them.

Libraries, museums and other organisations sometimes run writing workshops as part of a larger project. Often these will be centred around a collection, exhibition or piece of artwork – and quite frequently they're either free or cost just a few pounds. You'll need to read posters and get yourself on email lists to find out about these in time as, not surprisingly, spaces are filled quickly. I've been to several such events and have always created (and sold) a piece I'd never otherwise have written, so naturally I'm a fan of these.

> Make the most of workshops and conferences

Writing groups often run workshops, either led by one of the members, or someone they've invited in. Perhaps your group would like to try some of the exercises in this book – or even invite one of the authors along? We're very nice and jolly reasonable! If there are authors or creative writing teachers in your local area, they may be persuaded to run workshops tailored to meet the needs of your group. If their fee is split between you, it shouldn't be too expensive.

Don't worry if you're naturally a bit shy, or very nervous of reading your work out. Although you'll be encouraged to take part in discussions and perhaps offered feedback on your writing during workshops, you won't be forced into doing so. I expect that by the end you'll feel more comfortable about speaking out, but even if you don't, you can still benefit a great deal from the experience.

Whether there are good local workshops available or you have to travel or organise your own, I urge you to give them a try. You won't always create a saleable piece of work on the day, but the chances you'll gain something useful from the experience are very high. Having invested time and possibly money and being surrounded by other creative people is very motivating.

RJK: There are some very well-known longer courses that cover a wide range of writing subjects. The Winchester Writers' Festival runs at Winchester University for a weekend each June and the York Festival of Writing runs for a weekend in September, as does the weekend run by National Association of Writers' Groups (NAWG).

Then there are what are effectively writers' holidays, with Swanwick, for a week each August, being perhaps the best known in the UK. Look at the programmes of all of them and see which best fits your stage of writing before committing. Whichever you choose you will meet some wonderful people both amongst the tutors and fellow students.

SELF-PUBLISHING

Ebooks

The easiest way to self-publish your work is in ebook form. You can format your story or book using a standard word processing package and then use a programme such as Calibre (free to use but donations appreciated) to turn it into an ebook yourself for distribution. You also have the option to upload it to either Amazon, through their Kindle Direct Publishing (KDP) or a wider reaching portal such as Smashwords. You can also deal directly with the many ebook outlets for Apple, Barnes and Noble etc., but if you use Smashwords these will be covered that way.

Smashwords offer a 'style guide' which they present as being ebook best practice. (Amazon do something similar, but put less emphasis on it.) You will have to follow most of their guidelines in order for your book to be accepted into their 'Premium Catalogue' for wider distribution. However, although much of what they say is valid for all forms of epublishing they do not have a monopoly on knowing which presentation is correct, so don't feel obliged to follow everything they say.

> Start with a clean file when formatting work

It is worth putting your story into a clean unformatted word processing file, and then formatting it as you want from there. That will ensure you do not carry hidden formatting that has, to use a technical expression, become mangled as a result of all the changes you will inevitably have made while editing.

Remember to choose a font that works well when read on screen and look at other books you respect the layout of to see how you would like to format yours.

When formatting an ebook you need less 'white space' than in a print version. You also need to be aware that text flows onto a screen according to its size and therefore using a lot of indenting will not make it read easily, as it will go onto the next line rather too often. You need to use a layout that can give optimal presentation even on a small screen.

It is useful to learn how to build in bookmarks and hyperlinks to enable your reader to go to the chosen chapter or section. This is relatively straightforward once you find the right menu options in your word processing package.

You can pay a third party to do all this for you. If you go down that route, choose carefully and make sure you have seen a number of books they have formatted and not just the one they choose to send you. Cheap is not always best!

PC: It's really not that difficult to do yourself if you follow Rosemary's advice on formatting, given elsewhere in this book, and her suggestion to 'clean' the file before you start. Just don't try to do it in a hurry.

Turning your work into print

RJK: Your book is sitting in a file on the computer, or possibly you've got as far as issuing it as an ebook, but nagging away at the back of your mind is the thought 'I'd really like to hold a copy in my hands and turn the pages'. Besides that, your best friend wants a signed copy and your granny doesn't have an ereader.

In the past the solutions to this problem were limited and either required a significant outlay of capital or considerable technical understanding. With the advent of print-on-demand (POD) things started to change and with the launch of Createspace by Amazon the whole market changed. Now, anyone can have a printed copy of their book and with just a little time and effort it can look as good as any on the bookshelf. It can also be offered for sale, not only to your granny, but to a worldwide readership. There are other companies offering print-on-demand. Some of them charge an upfront fee and have a different pricing structure later. Createspace is very easy to use and for a small sales run is likely to work well.

Who is Createspace for?

Although it is tempting to say that Createspace is for anyone, there are constraints that need to be considered. If you want to sell your work commercially then you need a cover price that is viable, which precludes work greater than around 100,000 words, unless you are prepared to sacrifice earning royalties, or the overall appearance of the book. To produce something with commercial potential it works best at up to about 80,000 words. Also, at very low paginations it ceases to be viable commercially, but is still worth using to produce copies for friends and family.

```
Pros

    • Easiest way to global coverage
    • Easy process to follow
    • Good range of cover options
    • Works well 40,000 to 80,000 words
    • Generally good results
```

Things to do before you start

Whether you plan to sell your book commercially, or share it with your family, you want it to be of the highest standard possible. Before you think of converting it to book form, ensure your work is ready for publication. Editing and proof reading your manuscript are essential parts of the process. It is possible with a print-on-demand book through Createspace to alter the file after publication without cost, but there are constraints. An ISBN once issued relates to a book of a specific page length. If your changes alter the number of pages then you will need to start again as a new project. The other implication of making changes is that the book is off sale for a period of around 24 to 48 hours while the files go back through the approval process and are reissued to Amazon.

There are ISBN (International Standard Book Number) decisions to make before you go ahead. The ISBN is the way that your book will be differentiated from *Sheep Shearing in Outer Mongolia* or *Pirouetting Through the Pyrenees*. The arrangement of the numbers not only tells a stockist which book it is but also who the publisher is. If you look up the ISBN of this book you will find it is published by Alfie Dog Limited. The number is also specific to an edition, so there is no confusion. At the point of publication, the number becomes permanently attached to a specific number of pages, a page size and whether it is hardback or paperback.

Do you want Createspace to show as the publisher or do you want to set up your own imprint? If you are planning to publish other books you may benefit in buying a block of ISBNs from Nielsen if you are UK based. For a small quantity of numbers this is quite an expensive process and the options of a free ISBN from Createspace may be more appealing. Createspace offers greater flexibility of options to USA residents with the possibility of purchasing a single number from them that is then listed under your imprint. If you use Createspace's American ISBN numbers, you may find UK stores less willing to stock them. However, having your own ISBN will necessitate lodging copies with the UK Legal Deposit Libraries at your own expense. It is now possible to register to lodge the British Library copy electronically, but that is still not the case for the remaining reference locations which have to be complied with.

PC: It's possible to produce print copies of your book without bothering with an ISBN at all, but doing so severely limits the number of outlets where your book can be offered for sale and means libraries and physical bookstores are extremely unlikely to stock it.

Interior

RJK: When you start to set your project up in Createspace you will be asked to give your project a name. This is normally the book's title. Once you select create a 'paperback' you will choose between the 'Guided' or the 'Expert' options for set up. The guided option is relatively straightforward and will serve you well until you are completely happy with the process.

The first page deals with title information. The book's subtitle can be important if it is unclear from the title what the book will include. This description will appear on sales platforms to help guide purchasers. This is also the stage you add any authors' and editors' details and the name of any illustrators or other key people working on the project. Inclusion of names here makes registering the book for PLR an easier process for those involved; otherwise proof will be required of their contribution.

Dos

- Use a quality paperback as a guide for size and layout
- Take formatting your book at step at a time
- Take time to review the file for layout and consistency
- Take time to design an eye-catching cover
- Make sure blank pages are correctly treated

Page size

If you want to sell your work commercially, one of the most important decisions you will make is what size paper to use. The size which is 'recommended' by Createspace as the most common is 6″ x 9″. However, in the UK, if you pick up any paperback off your bookshelf there are only a small minority of novels which are that size. It may be a more economical layout, in terms of reducing the number of pages requiring printing, and if that is your primary consideration then it may be perfectly adequate. If you want your book to be stocked in bookshops alongside other titles and you want it to look at home on any bookshelf, then the best approach is to select a book from your shelf and use it as your guide. You can use that paperback as a guide for other stages in the process. Try to make sure the book you have selected is from a respected publisher rather than another that has been self-published. Createspace do offer templates for a wide range of page sizes and although some have restrictions on distribution, this mostly affects USA options only. Bear in mind the size of fiction paperbacks differs from many non-fiction books. Reference books, of all types, including this one are often of a larger size.

Paper colour

Some industry professionals will tell you that for your book to be taken seriously, you need to use cream coloured paper. This is because historically paperbacks were printed on the cheapest stock of paper which was of sufficient grade and that was generally cream in colour. The cream of Createspace's paper is not the same as old paperbacks on your shelf. For a start it is a different grade of paper with a smoother finish. Whichever you choose it will not look quite the same as a standard paperback. The paper used for short run digital printing does appear slightly different to that used on longer run presses. White paper can be easier to read as it gives greater contrast to the print.

Layout

Formatting your book for printing is the hardest stage of the process. You can upload the file you have prepared already, as long as you have set the correct paper size and margins for the work. The margins will vary according to the number of pages your book makes, with the inner margin being slightly wider to allow for increased loss of visibility of the inside edge of the page for higher numbers of pages. Createspace offer templates, for each page size, to which you can add your work. These include the correct margin settings, as well as having pages laid out ready for each section of your book. However, whether you use a Createspace template or your own file you need to consider the following points in addition to the margins.

If you take the professionally published paperback you are using as your guide you will notice a number of things:

Headers and footers

The page headers differ according to whether the page is a left-hand or right-hand page. In the templates this is already allowed for and you will slot in your book title on one side and the author name on the other. The template is also set up so that no header appears on the first page of a chapter. One point to watch is that the template has only ten chapters. If you want more than this, you will need to use a section break rather than a page break to maintain the pattern of headers. (For some books you may wish to use the chapter name as a header for each section, you can do this by 'unlinking' the header from the previous section, so that it stands alone.)

The footers will normally include only the page number. If there are pages that you do not wish the page number to appear on, such as a page at the back listing your other books, then you will need a new section which you then unlink from the previous one before deleting the page number.

Front matter

The Createspace templates include pages for the 'front matter' of the book. That is the section containing the title page, the title verso, acknowledgements, dedication and contents. It is not necessary to have all of these and they can be removed if not required. However, the title verso (rear of the title page) should contain the copyright information and ISBN. The Createspace template contains minimal copyright information. It is worth including a fuller copyright statement to ensure that all types of usage have been covered.

If you look at a professionally printed book, then you will notice that some pages are deliberately left blank. This is for two reasons. Firstly, and importantly, it is so that key pages are always set on a right-hand page, to which the eye is drawn, rather than on the left. In particular, the first chapter of the book will almost certainly start on a right-hand page. The second reason for books printed on traditional presses is that the press can normally only print in multiples of sixteen pages, so a book running to 300 pages of print will contain 304 pages with four blanks. With digital printing blank pages are more an aesthetic choice, as the presses do not have the same constraints.

One of the biggest problems with the Createspace templates is how blank pages are treated. Simply inserting a blank page can lead to that page not being recognised in their initial review procedure, which will not only throw out all your other pages but also upset the margin configuration. You may find yourself resubmitting the file several times in order to force the recognition of the blank page. It seems that creating it as a section and then removing the header and footer details is the most effective way to ensure their process 'sees' the page as existing.

New chapters

How far down a page each chapter starts is a matter of presentational preference. Normally a new chapter starts a new page and there are a few lines of blank space before the title of the chapter. If you want to use fewer pages, then it is possible to run one chapter on after the previous one. The other key point to consider is the overall layout. When you come to review the file you may find you have chapters finishing with a single line of text on a page. It is better to try to reduce the instances where this happens, particularly if it involves turning a page to find the last word or line of the chapter. It is less of an issue where the single line goes onto a right-hand page as the reader will be able to see that at the same time as the rest of the paragraph.

PC: It really does look peculiar, and amateurish, to have just one or two lines on the page. Either edit the chapter a little to avoid this, or start the next chapter on the same page.

RJK: Traditionally the first paragraph of a chapter is not indented, but subsequent paragraphs are. The same is true where a space is left to denote a break in the scene within a chapter. The Createspace template is set for the chapter start, but will not recognise a scene break. Be careful in copying your work across that you do not copy the formatting from your original file. Select the 'merge formatting' option when pasting text so that you preserve aspects such as italics, but do not corrupt the format of the template. The Createspace templates use Garamond as the font. The other fonts commonly used in printing are Times New Roman or Palatino Linotype. All three of these look good on the printed page and are relatively easy to read. Some modern fonts, whilst working well on screen, are less effective in print.

> Don'ts
> - Forget to use section breaks instead of page breaks for extra chapters
> - Rush through any of the stages
> - Forget to allow suitable margins
> - Expect a book over 100,000 words to be commercially viable
> - Order more than £135 of books at a time

Review

Once all this is complete and the interior of the book is submitted you will have the opportunity to review your files. Do not take anything for granted. Even using a Createspace template you can find that, for no apparent reason, the print area has shrunk and your text is surrounded by a large amount of white space. Re-uploading the file usually clears this problem. Look for consistency in all aspects of your layout, if you have used any symbol to split changes of scene make sure they are correctly aligned in all cases. Do not assume that any formatting you did in your original document will have copied across to the Createspace template correctly. It is safest to review all pages.

Cover

Having completed the interior of your book then you will move on to the cover. There are two options for your cover depending on your level of experience. For the more experienced there is the option to upload a completed cover using a pdf. The necessary sizes allowing for bleeds and spine are available in the help facilities on the site. The easier approach is to use the Cover Creator, which still allows for different levels of preparation on your part.

You can choose a design and images from Createspace and follow the step by step guide to building your cover. If you want to upload your own images into the templates that is straightforward following their guidelines and remembering that images need to be 300dpi. Be sure you have the right to use your chosen image.

As Createspace titles sell at different prices in different countries they do not normally show the price. The bar code with the ISBN will be dropped into place for you by Createspace, however it is important to leave that area of the back cover free. It will become apparent when you review your cover if you have not left a sufficiently large area.

Checking and proofing

Once all steps have been completed your project is submitted for final review of the proof copy. The proof is best viewed in hard copy, but given the cost and time of shipping this may be difficult. There are also the options to review on screen or as a pdf.

Selling your book

With Createspace, you can make your book available through Amazon in the UK, Europe and the US as well as other parts of the world. You choose the selling price on each site. Your royalty will be:

Royalty = Retail Price – (Createspace basic cost + Amazon mark-up)

For every £1 you add to the retail price only 60p appears in the royalty box, the remaining 40p will be the additional Amazon commission. Although this seems a high percentage, it is lower than the percentage you would need to give to supply Amazon directly with paperbacks if you have your books printed elsewhere.

Wider distribution of paperbacks in the UK is not easily achieved through Createspace. It is possible for USA markets at a premium (a lower royalty to you). You will find other online retailers offering your book for sale, but they will source these direct through Createspace only when they receive an order.

You also have the option to convert the book for Kindle publication, rather than doing this separately through Amazon.

What can possibly go wrong?

The whole process is relatively straightforward, but it is not without its pitfalls. Some of those are entirely within your control and some are ones you can do little about.

Cons

- Colour quality unreliable
- Royalties / sales difficult to track
- Uneconomic over about 100,000 words
- Delivery can take six weeks
- Problem resolution is poor

You cannot fix your launch date

There is no facility within Createspace to fix your launch date or to buy copies direct from them at wholesale prices ahead of your launch. With the exception of your proof copy, you cannot buy copies until the project has gone live. Timing a project to a specific date is not easy, there is a time delay between your book being live on Createspace and it appearing on Amazon. This can vary from hours to days and as the Amazon sites operate independently of each other it will not appear at exactly the same time on all of them.

Buying direct from Createspace

If you are looking to sell your book commercially you may want to buy in bulk from Createspace. Bearing in mind that Createspace is likely to ship to you from outside the EU, there are two problems. Firstly, the shipping cost is about the same amount as the books, even if you go for the slowest option which takes up to six weeks. Secondly, you need to keep the order below the level for import duties to be levied. There is no VAT on books so the threshold at which duty, and duty collection charges, apply is currently £135. Given the fluctuation in exchange rates it is best to allow a margin within this figure.

Packaging of bulk purchases is not great, so don't be surprised if a few copies of your order are a little bent; although this appears to be a greater problem buying through Amazon than direct through Createspace.

If you need books quickly, you can reduce the book price and wait for the reduction to filter through to Amazon, and then order from Amazon with free delivery and a shorter delivery time. However, you cannot guarantee that others will not also benefit from the lower price and you lose royalties in the process. Do remember to reset the price as soon as your order is confirmed.

Selling through Amazon

Createspace print through a number of facilities and offer your book for sale through Amazon in the USA, UK and around Europe. Anyone buying outside these regions will need to go to their 'nearest' Amazon site. If you have friends around the world, sending out a single link it can be difficult to avoid inadvertently causing them to incur high postage charges.

Selling through outlets other than Amazon

If you receive requests for your book in the UK from wholesalers or bookstores they will expect a significant discount on the cover price (between 40% and 55%). If you source books in bulk from Createspace in America this may be possible, but it is difficult to achieve on a print-on-demand book without making the cover price uneconomic. You may be able to agree a lower discount with small outlets in your area, particularly if you manage to generate publicity around your book launch.

Print quality

If you use a commercial printer and the print quality is poor, then you can speak with the printer and normally receive some recompense. When working with Createspace you do not have any personal relationship with the company and this is most noticeable when problems arise.

Conclusion

Although print-on-demand was available before Createspace, as with many Amazon projects it has utterly changed the industry. Whilst not without its difficulties, Createspace is by far the easiest way for an individual or small publisher to achieve almost global coverage with a paperback. The setup process is more cost effective for low volume sales and easier to follow. Even as you move towards mainstream printing it is more cost effective to continue to produce a Createspace edition to fulfil Amazon sales in both the UK and abroad than it is to supply Amazon directly, or achieve the sales direct through other outlets.

PUBLIC SPEAKING

PC: I used to be very shy and my natural speaking voice is quiet, so I can easily understand the concern many people have over speaking in public. You don't actually need to read your work to others, give talks or run classes, be interviewed on the radio, or tell anyone you write, but you'll almost certainly be more successful if you do. Speaking up in classes and reading out work for feedback will be helpful in learning the craft of writing, but the biggest advantage of public speaking is in the promotion of our work. Simply put, if we don't find a way to tell people we've written books, they won't buy them.

> Public speaking promotes your writing

Knowing that becoming better at public speaking would be an advantage to me as a writer wasn't the main reason for applying for my last job, but it was a factor. For five years I worked as a tour guide (on HMS Victory, in Portsmouth.) I doubt you'll want to do anything quite as drastic, so I'll just pass on some of the things I learned.

The most important thing is that your audience must be able to hear and understand you. Manage that and you're 90% of the way to being an excellent public speaker. There's no point giving out useful information, being fascinating or witty if no one has a clue what you're saying. If there's no microphone, speak as loudly as you can without yelling (although yelling is better than not being heard). It helps to look at the person furthest away from you and address part of your talk directly to them. You also need to speak quite slowly. More slowly than will feel natural. If you're nervous there's a tendency to rush through to get it over with, which makes your words hard to follow. Remember too, that your accent may be difficult for some people to understand.

Practice beforehand, speaking aloud. Reading silently is not the same at all. If possible, address the talk to a friend, who is standing as far away as you expect the most distant of your audience to be and get them to gesture when you need to be louder or slower.

RJK: If you can get access to a village hall or similar, use it to practice projecting your voice. To make your voice carry you may need to let it be deeper and try to breathe deeply while speaking, so you don't start to run out of breath and speed up. Speak from the depths of your diaphragm to help your voice to carry without shouting.

PC: If you stumble over any words or phrases change them (unless giving a reading of already published work.) Mark in where you need to emphasise anything, or pause for effect.

RJK: Even if work is already published there is no harm in slight word or comma changes to make it easy to read aloud. It is actually a good tip when editing your work to read it aloud as you will very soon pick up all the places where small improvements can be made. This is essential if your work is going to be recorded for audio. Having your narrator slip up and convey the wrong meaning because of a misplaced comma will not make it easy for the listener.

> Ensure your writing reads easily

PC: Other than specifically reading passages of your work, don't read a prepared script. It feels impersonal and is therefore less engaging. If you can, it's better to speak (apparently) spontaneously, perhaps prompted by brief notes. You may like to take a more detailed back-up script the first few times in case nerves get the better of you. Reading your notes is a lot better than drying up completely.

RJK: Don't be afraid to keep a copy of your cv handy to check back on. We all have times where we completely forget when asked a question. It's better to be able to glance at a crib sheet to check what date your novel was published than to come out with something that makes no sense.

PC: If speaking to a large group, pick out a few individuals – one on the left, right, back, centre and front of the room – and speak to them in turn. It feels less daunting to cope with five people and you'll give the impression of treating your audience as individuals.

> Practice projecting your voice

RJK: If you are speaking to a large room, look just over the heads of people and it looks as though you are looking at everyone. It will also help you to project your voice.

PC: Should you make a mistake, only correct yourself if absolutely necessary. The audience won't realise you'd planned to use a different phrase, or say things in a different order. Constant apologies, or virtual repeats of the same points are very irritating. Likewise, don't get off to a bad start by running yourself or your material down before you get going.

RJK: I was brought up on the adage 'if you say something with enough conviction then people will believe you' and it's true. The times you won't convince anyone are the ones you get tongue tied or apologise for yourself and your inadequacies.

PC: A good way to engage with the audience is to invite questions. They too may be a little shy at first, so you could have somebody primed to start this off should everyone else be quiet, or be ready with something like, 'I'm often asked…' That gives you free reign to talk about anything you like. Don't feel pressurised into answering every question. If you don't know, then admit the fact – perhaps asking if anyone else does. If a question is personal e.g. 'how much money do you earn?' or 'how do you research the sex scenes?' then you're entitled not to answer, but try to do so without belittling the questioner.

RJK: If there really are no questions then have a wrap up prepared along the lines of; 'That's good, I've obviously covered all you need to know.' That way instead of finishing with an embarrassed silence you end with a confident note.

When in front of a room of people, in order to look and feel confident, stand with both feet squarely on the ground. Do not move from leg to leg or find you are standing on one leg while twisting the other round the back of your stationary leg. Keep your hands still too. If necessary hold a piece of paper, but hold it firmly and don't start twisting it or pulling bits off. And SMILE! It is very easy when we are nervous to look down and look worried.

Look ahead, hold your head up and smile – not a nervous smile accompanied by lots of giggling, but just a straightforward, confident, 'I know my subject' smile.

Radio interviews

PC: These are a little harder to prepare for, as they tend to be unrehearsed. You can guess likely questions though. For example, if you've been invited onto the show because you've just had a book published, you'll probably be asked what it's called and what it's about. Think in advance about what you'd like to say, but be guided by the questions too. If it's a local radio station they'll be interested in any local 'angle' such as where it's set, or the author's home town.

> Take a copy of your book

You might find it helpful to take a copy of your book with you, both to remind you why you're there and so you can read off the title and your own name should your mind go completely blank!

RJK: It's also nice to leave the presenter with a copy in the hope they might read it and mention it again. Reread your synopsis before you go in, to help make sure the storyline is very fresh in your mind. It's quite possible you're half way through writing your next book and you don't want to get the two confused.

PC: These interviews are more like friendly chats than interrogations (although I admit they don't feel that way until after the first one is finished). It's to the host's advantage to have interesting guests, so they'll rescue you if you start to flounder or dry up.

RJK: If your next novel comes up, don't find yourself being cornered into giving a publication date for it when you're still only part way through. I'm speaking from the experience here of my first radio interview. I had to work very hard when I got home as I then felt obliged to meet the deadline I'd given.

Reading your own work

PC: The advantage with this is you know exactly what you're going to say and can practice as much as you like. If necessary make small changes so reading is easier, but don't keep fiddling about with it so you don't know where you are.

If possible, print out the work using a large clear font. Hold the book or sheets so they don't cover your face. It's more polite and engaging if you look at your audience, plus it often helps people to understand if they can see your expressions. Clearly mark where you want to pause or emphasise a point. Try to memorise some sections, so you can look up at your audience as much as possible.

RJK: With practice you can learn to read ahead of what you are saying, so that the next sentence is in your head and you can look up from time to time to see your audience. If you do this it is also easier to put appropriate emotion into sections and, where appropriate, use different voices for your characters.

> **Learn to read ahead**

Once you become confident you may be able to get engagements speaking to WI groups or other meetings. Most are only too happy to find a good speaker and you may be able to sell your work as well as earning a fee. If you do that, what works well is to intersperse reading your work with giving the background story to how it came about. It can be huge fun.

OUR TYPICAL WRITING DAYS

Patsy's 'typical' day

PC: I started writing during an unsettled part of my life. For the first few years, I moved home four times and had five different jobs. My writing was done on trains, ships and buses, in lunch breaks, evenings and at one point I had weekends free so wrote then too. Luckily I'm not keen on routine, so it wasn't a problem for me. Now, even more luckily, I am able to write full-time.

For me there are writing days and non-writing days and these are further divided into at home or away in the campervan days. As this is a book about writing I'll concentrate on the writing ones.

About half my writing is done in a home office, which I share with my husband. His desk is the tidy one. I have a proper, supportive office chair. The monitor, cordless keyboard and mouse are nicely set up so I'm not putting unnecessary strain on my eyes or joints. My laptop connects up to these, the printer, and a hard drive which automatically backs-up as I work.

For about half my time, I'm in the campervan. (It's not all holidays – Gary travels a lot with work and I go too and write.) In the van, I use the same laptop and back-up to a separate hard drive. I write either sprawled out in the back, or hunched over the low table.

Both at home or in the van, I tend to wake up first. Sometimes I immediately know what I want to write. This may be because I have something I've already started, an outline to work to, or a non-fiction deadline to meet. On other occasions, I'll mentally plot out an idea – a sort of deliberate daydream. I then get out of bed, make a pot of tea and write. Depending on what I'm writing and how much, if any, is already done this lasts from thirty minutes to over four hours. My aim is to keep going forward until I come to the end of the story, article, scene or whatever. If I realise I need to change something from earlier, need to research, or get stuck on one part, I make a note and move on.

Once that is done, I speak to Gary and make more tea. (If I've been writing for a while, he'll be working too and will have brought me tea, which I'll have drunk without noticing.) After that, I need a break from actual writing and either do writing related tasks such as formatting work, promotion, submissions, research, or walk down to the beach for the rest of the morning. Or if we're in the van we might visit a castle or look round a garden.

In the afternoon, I usually either redraft something (not normally the piece I wrote in the morning, but if it's urgent I might) or edit. If I'm editing, I will have given myself a break from that piece either by leaving it for several days (months in the case of novels) or writing something else. Generally, it's both. Sometimes I'll do more initial writing. That's most likely to happen if I'm working on a longer piece which remains unfinished from the morning.

I now very rarely write in the evenings. I'm much more likely to read, engage in social media, blog, read friends' work and critique it, carry out admin – or perhaps do nothing writing related.

There are exceptions. Gary's photography quite often happens early in the morning and I frequently go with him. On those occasions I either start the whole routine later, or miss out the first phase. Now and again, I just don't feel like writing, or redrafting, or admin and will skip that bit. Sometimes I have a deadline to meet, or am so absorbed in a project I'll work on it for most of the day. Weather plays a part too, particularly when we're in the van. You won't be shocked to hear that if it's raining or cold and windy, I'm far more likely to stay in and work. In good weather spent at interesting locations I'll write less and spend more time on other sorts of fun, but I'm not happy if I go for more than a few days without writing.

On non-writing days, which are usually the result of some other commitment, I don't write or redraft or edit. I'll probably still carry out some writing related work though. However busy we are with other things, there's usually time to open the post or check emails and note the fate of submissions into our records, to look up a few facts or stock up on stamps.

Rosemary's writing routine

RJK: As with Patsy I do have the luxury of being a full-time writer and publisher, but I wasn't when I started. I am a writing compulsive. I have to write and being without a pen and paper when I want to write something down would be a dreadful realisation. I write many notes by emailing them to myself using my phone or adding them to my to do list on the phone, but I've invariably got a pen and paper in my bag as well.

I've enjoyed many travel trips alone over the years, by writing down all my observations, rather than having someone to tell. Our loft is full of notebooks filled with odd views of the world. I've written on planes, on trains and even had to pull into service stations to write a couple of lines down before I forget them.

Now my day looks a little like this:

Whenever the dogs get me up, usually before six, I'll let them out then go to my desk to answer the overnight emails. It's one of the downsides of working with insomniacs and people in different time zones. Generally, that takes me up to breakfast and showering. After that I'm a juggler. I rarely sit and spend several hours on the same project. Particularly if I'm editing, either my own work or someone else's, I find I'm most effective working in chunks of intense concentration of no more than about half an hour at a time. I write in chunks too. Usually these are interspersed with dog walking. Dog walking is either used for planning what I'm going to write or to clear my head for the next task.

If I have a scene to write for a fiction story, whilst I walk I visualise what is happening and try to tune in to what the characters want to say to each other. I'm lucky, I have a very good memory and can remember whole conversations that the characters have this way. If they have too much to say, and I fear forgetting it, then I either use the voice memo on the phone as I walk or ring my own house voicemail and leave a message for when I get back.

I cannot write more than one story at the same time, but I can have stories or books at different development stages without finding that they merge into each other. I'm usually working on at least three or four things at once. Researching a project, writing something, editing a different piece of work and setting a book or cover design for another. This approach would not work for everyone, but if I were to try to spend too many hours on one thing I'd probably get bored. By later in the day I'll do any computer work, site maintenance and general admin. There are also things like my own newsletter, blog posts and accounts which are done at intervals as they crop up on my rather extensive to do list.

In amongst all that I'll fit helping the dog write his blog and the usual things around the house, which, when your office is at home, everyone assumes you have time for. In many ways, I'm really not an example to follow. I'm a workaholic and can often be found at my desk until much later into the evening than is sociable. I'm just fortunate to have an understanding family.

***

As you find your own writing pattern and develop your style, we both wish you every success and would be delighted to hear about your progress, especially if we've been able to help in some way. We'd also be delighted if you could spare the time to leave us a review on Amazon or Goodreads.

FAQS

A publisher likes my book, but wants me to help towards the costs. Is this normal?

It's becoming more so! Although not always the case, the request for authors to pay out, rather than the offer to pay them, very often indicates a scam. Generally, the up-front costs you'd face when self-publishing (editing, proofreading, cover design etc.) will be met by a publisher, should they decide to take you on.

If the publisher has recouped their costs from the author before publication, then there's little incentive for them to put effort into selling the books. Do a search online and in local bookshops. Can you find any by this publisher? Do they seem to be selling? Also the website Preditors and Editors is worth looking at for publishers who are not recommended.

If you're going to have to pay to get your book published, might you be better off self-publishing and keeping all the profit for yourself? Although you may still want to pay out for some of the services that a publisher would normally provide.

The editor obviously didn't understand my story, or didn't read it properly. What should I do?

Write one they will understand, or which they'll want to read right to the end!

A piece of writing will be rejected if it doesn't fit the publication's requirements. If it's the wrong length, tone, genre or sent too late, then they can't use it even if it really is brilliant. Of course, they may have got confused or bored because it isn't written as well as it could be. Look through it again and see if it can be improved before you try it somewhere else.

Don't try arguing with them about it! You may want to submit to them again in the future.

I keep seeing the same author names in the magazines I read, shouldn't they stop submitting and give others a chance?

No. Would you?

If you frequently see work by the same author it will be for one reason only – they write work which meets the publisher's standards. If you do the same, you'll sell your stories too.

What is a writing cv and do I need one?

It's a record of you writing successes, usually publication of work or having been placed in a competition, relevant experience, and possibly qualifications.

Usually you don't need them. No publisher will turn down a book which they believe could make them money, or refuse to publish a short story perfect for their magazine just because you've not boasted of previous success.

In the case of short fiction, they're no help at all as the piece is judged on its own merits. A good track record may help convince a book publisher that you're not a one hit wonder and that might make a difference in your favour. With articles or non-fiction books, then you'll need a qualification or experience to show that you can write the piece.

Do I have to have sex scenes for my book to sell?

No. Not unless you're promoting it as a sizzling, passionate read. If you'd like to write about sex and it fits into your chosen genre and storyline, then feel free to include it. If you'd rather not, or it doesn't fit naturally into the book, then it's better to leave it out. The same goes for violence and swearing.

Why do readers say my storylines aren't believable? These things really happened to me or people I know.

Real life can be very strange. If you write the things that actually happen, they can seem too extreme even if they are real. We've all heard the saying 'truth is stranger than fiction' and if you've lived through some of the odder coincidences that can occur, then you'll see why. Put those on the written page and readers may see them as contrived or unlikely, however real they are.

When we make up the entire story, we make sure our plotlines and character reactions are plausible. If we are writing about real events, we sometimes take less care over plausibility as we know it can, or did, happen just as we've written it.

GLOSSARY

ALCS – Authors' Licensing and Collecting Society. www.alcs.co.uk. This organisation collects money due to an author where others have used their work, be it for photocopying or other reproduction in education etc. You'll need to register, and then add in every qualifying book, story and article you have published. There's a £25 fee which is taken from your earnings, you don't pay them anything directly. Payments vary according to what you've had published and where. We strongly recommend registering.

Acknowledgements – You may wish to acknowledge those who've helped with your book, e.g. with research or by allowing the use of material subject to copyright. If used, this page may appear either at the front, or back, of the book.

Advance – An amount of royalties paid by a publisher to an author in anticipation of sales. The actual royalties earned are offset against this before any further payment is made.

ARE – Alternative rational explanation. This is when, in ghost/sixth sense stories, the reader is offered an alternative to the supernatural explanation e.g. the face of the murdered man appears on the killer's bedroom wall – but the roof leaks so it could just be a damp patch. The reader is left to make up their own mind.

Blurb – A few lines, often on the back cover of a book, to encourage people to read on. It may be in the form of a brief description of the story, but will not include the whole plot. Often it will include questions as a teaser to the story.

Commissioned submission – This is where the author has been asked to produce a particular piece of work, possibly after sending a pitch. Often subject, word length and due date have been previously agreed.

Covering letter – A letter accompanying a submission. It will include the author's contact details as well as the details of the story (title, length, genre). May also include details of rights offered or the fact the story has been published before. Check submission guidelines to see what is required.

Dedication – You can, if you wish, dedicate your book to an individual, or several people. This will be done on a separate page at the front of the book.

Digital first – Literally this means producing an ebook before the print version. In practice, it usually means only producing the e-version. Digital publication incurs lower costs than a traditional print run, so publishers can take more risks with unknown authors. Often these companies are part of a bigger publishing company. In that case, ebooks which do well might then be released as paperbacks, but there's no guarantee of that.

Draft – A version of a piece of writing. The first is the 'rough draft'. This is likely to go through many revisions, or drafts, before the piece is ready for submission.

Exclusive rights – Only the person or organisation who acquires these rights can use the work in the way specified.

Fillers – Small pieces which aren't full length articles, stories, or adverts. They are often supplied by readers and in the case of national magazines there's usually some payment offered. Letters to the editor, tips, anecdotes, brief news items and jokes may be considered, depending on the publication. They're a good way for a beginner author to achieve their first success.

Flat fee – A set amount paid for a piece of work. Usually for short stories or articles, but can also be for books. The author will receive the agreed amount no matter how many, or few, copies are sold.

HEA – Happy ever after.

HFN – Happy for now. Usually where the problem hasn't been entirely resolved, but we see the character is beginning to move on or come to terms with the issue.

House style – Each publication will make decisions on how work is presented and will adhere to these no matter what the author's preferred style. This will be things such as whether to use single or double quotes for speech, if paragraphs should be indented or not, whether they prefer present or past tense. Submitting work which conforms to the house style makes things easier for editors and shows that you've properly studied the market you're submitting to.

ISBN – International Standard Book Number – A unique number given to a book to identify it. These are purchased by publishers from the relevant distributor in each country and allocated by the publisher to all books published under their publishing imprint. Each format of a book requires a different number and a new number would need to be allocated if in any subsequent changes to the number of pages in the printed book or the size of the printed book changed. It also needs a new number if the book moves to a different publisher.

MSS – Manuscript. The document which contains the story, book, article etc. May be paper or electronic.

Multiple submissions – Sending more than one piece to the same publisher. Fine as long as their guidelines allow this, but don't swamp them. There's no point sending more than they can possibly use, plus all your work may be unsuitable in the same way, for that market. Better to send just a few and await a reply before trying again.

Narrative voice – Tone and style in which a piece is written. An author, may over time develop a particular style by which their work is recognised. This is built from word length, sentence structures, punctuation choices and the cadence of their writing style. For some it can be recognised consistently from story to story, while for others not only might it develop over time, but vary by subject area or genre. The narrative voice should suit the style of the book. E.g. a children's story should be more simple and straightforward than adult fiction.

Non-exclusive rights – A person, or organisation, will acquire the rights to use the material in the specified way, but the rights may also be offered to others, or used by the author.

Pitch – This is an offer to write a particular piece, usually non-fiction. You'll need to explain what you'd like to write, how you intend to tackle the subject and why you're a good person to do this.

PLR – Public Lending Rights can be earned by authors when their books are borrowed from a public library. It's about seven pence per loan. The author needs to register their books for PLR, which is easy and free. In order to qualify, those books then need to be in the libraries from which sample figures are gathered. The sample changes annually, so it's worth registering even if you don't expect to qualify straight away. www.plr.uk.com This covers the UK and Ireland. Many other countries have an equivalent system.

POV – Point of view (see relevant book section).

Query – A request for permission to submit work to somewhere which states they do not consider unsolicited manuscripts. Can also mean to chase up submissions you've not heard back about.

Royalties – An amount earned by an author for sales of their work. It is usually part of the profit (net) or sale price (gross) from the sale of a book or story which is made to the author, by the publisher. Often it will be as a percentage rather than set amount. The amount due should have been agreed in advance. They may be on a sliding scale – lower at first, then higher once initial costs have been covered, or dependent on the gross selling price of the book.

SAE – Stamped addressed envelope.

Sans serif font – Fonts such as Calibri which do not have serifs (lines) on the arms of the characters.

Scene – A section of a story which happens in one location (unless it's a chase scene!) and time period, and deals with one incident.

Section break – A blank line in a document used to indicate a change or pause. May be used to show a jump in time, new location, or a change of POV character. In setting a book it refers to the start of a new page which represents a new section of the book.

Serif font – Fonts such as Times New Roman which have lines topping and tailing the arms of the characters.

Simultaneous submission – Sending the same piece of work to more than one potential publisher. With books this is common practice. With short stories and articles it's a really bad idea.

SPAG – Spelling, punctuation and grammar.

Speculative submission (On spec) – Where an author submits work which has not been requested. Most work for women's magazines is submitted in this way.

Submission – Any work offered for consideration.

Subplot – An 'extra' storyline. For example, in a murder mystery, solving the crime will be the main plot, but there may be a subplot involving the detective's love life or hobby.

Synopsis – A brief description of the entire work, including the ending.

TAB – *Take a Break* – A weekly women's magazine.

TABFF – *Take a Break's Fiction Feast* – A monthly magazine containing twenty short stories.

Title page – In a book this is simply the page with the title on (and generally little else). In the case of a submission, or competition entry, it's a separate sheet bearing the story's title and generally the author's contact details – but do check what's required. This will be mentioned in the guidelines or rules. When submissions were always made on paper this was where an editor might make notes about the work. They're often not needed now.

Title verso – A page usually on the reverse of the title page covering the legal requirements of ISBN, copyright notice, publisher and printer.

TPF – *The People's Friend* – A weekly magazine containing fiction.

TWN – *The Weekly News* – A weekly newspaper, similar in style to a women's magazine. Contains fiction.

Unreliable narrator – A viewpoint character who gives information as fact, but is actually wrong or misleading. They may be lying (e.g. in twist ending crime stories where they're revealed to be the murderer) or fantasising (e.g. Walter Mitty) or not know the whole truth (e.g. a child). You will need to give the reader some clues about this.

Womag – Women's magazine.

Work in progress (WIP) – Whatever you're currently working on, more commonly used to describe a longer project such as a serial or novel rather than a short story. Unfinished pieces of work in general.

WW – *Woman's Weekly* – A weekly women's magazine, containing short stories and a serial.

WWFS – *Woman's Weekly Fiction Special* – A monthly magazine containing twenty short stories.

USEFUL RESOURCES

- Competitions that are free to enter www.patsy-collins.blogspot.com

- Historical news reports www.britishpathe.com

- Intellectual property blog dearrichblog.blogspot.co.uk

- ISBN – in the UK www.isbn.nielsenbook.co.uk in the USA www.isbn.org

- Names – history and origin www.behindthename.com

- National Novel Writing Month nanowrimo.org

- Plagiarism www.dustball.com/cs/plagiarism.checker

- Short story anthology calls for submissions thejohnfox.com/publishers-of-short-story-collections

- Short story magazine and competition listings www.christopherfielden.com

- Submissions information www.duotrope.com

- Telephone numbers which can be used for fiction stakeholders.ofcom.org.uk/telecoms/numbering/guidance-tele-no/numbers-for-drama

- Timeline calculator to ensure your plot timing works wendyswritingnow.blogspot.co.uk/2013/09/wendys-story-timeline-version-2-with.html

- Urban myths and legends www.snopes.com

- Womag news and information including guidelines www.womagwriter.blogspot.co.uk

- Writers' & Artists' Yearbook www.writersandartists.co.uk

- Writers' Forum Magazine www.writers-forum.com

- Writing exercises writingexercises.co.uk/index.php

- Writing Magazine – incorporating Writers' News www.writers-online.co.uk

OTHER BOOKS BY THE AUTHORS

Patsy Collins

Short story collections

Not A Drop To Drink (Free ebook)
Up The Garden Path
Over The Garden Fence
Through The Garden Gate
No Family Secrets

Novels

Paint Me A Picture
Firestarter
Escape To The Country
A Year And A Day

Rosemary J. Kind

Novels

The Appearance of Truth
The Lifetracer
Alfie's Woods

Humour

Alfie's Diary
Lovers Take Up Less Space
Pet Dogs Democratic Party Manifesto

Non-fiction

Negotiation Skills for Lawyers

Alfie Dog Fiction

Taking your imagination for a walk

For hundreds of short stories, collections and novels visit our
website at www.alfiedog.com

Join us on Facebook
www.facebook.com/AlfieDogLimited

16078212R00163

Printed in Poland
by Amazon Fulfillment
Poland Sp. z o.o., Wrocław